Allyear Tax Guide 304

YOUR EXECUTOR DUTIES

by

Holmes F. Crouch
Tax Specialist

Published by

ROBERT ERDMANN PUBLISHING
28629 Meadow Glen Way West
Escondido, CA 92026

ISBN 0-945339-14-3

Library of Congress 90-082813

Printed in U.S.A.
90-0123456789

Publication 304

YOUR EXECUTOR DUTIES

———————

Series 300
Retirees and Estates

Allyear Tax Guides

Other tax subjects in our 25-title series are listed on the last page of this book.

PREFACE

If you are a *professional-level* **taxpayer,** this book can be helpful to you. It is designed to be read — from cover to cover — in less than six hours. Or, you can skim read it in approximately 30 minutes.

Either way, you are treated to **tax knowledge** . . . *beyond the ordinary.* The "beyond" is that which you cannot find in official instructions, and that which is not ordinarily imparted to you by professional counselors.

Taxpayers have different levels of interest in a selected tax subject. For this reason, this book starts with introductory fundamentals and progresses through some rather complex situations. You can verify the progression by chapter and section in the table of contents. In the text, "applicable law" is quoted in pertinent part. Key interpretive phrases and key tax forms are emphasized. Real-life examples are given . . . in down-to-earth style.

This book has 12 chapters. This number provides depth without cross-subject rambling. Each chapter starts with a head summary of meaningful information.

To overcome the humdrum of ordinary tax jargon, informative diagrams and tables are placed strategically throughout the text. Most of the illustrations are true originals. By leafing through page by page, reading the summaries and section headings, and glancing at the diagrams and tables, you can get a good handle on the matters covered.

Effort has been made to update and incorporate all of the latest tax law changes that are significant to the title subject. However, "beyond the ordinary" does not encompass every conceivable variant of fact and law that might give rise to protracted dispute and litigation. Consequently, if a particular statement or paragraph is crucial to your own specific case, you are urged to seek professional counseling. Otherwise, the information presented is general and is designed for a broad range of reader interests.

The Author

INTRODUCTION

If you have been named and appointed as an Executor/Executrix in someone's will — or if you expect to be so appointed — this book is for you.

This book also is for anyone who has written a will, and who wants the appointee therein to become familiar with duties he/she is to perform after your death. There are many such duties which are not well publicized. Most will-appointed executors undergo the experience only once or twice in a lifetime.

An executor is a person who carries out — "executes" — the Last Will and Testament of a decedent. Thus, an executor is the *personal representative* of a deceased person. In such capacity, an executor is fully responsible for implementing the decedent's intention regarding the accounting for, and distribution of, his/her estate. An executor is also responsible for minimizing the depletion of an estate through death taxes, attorney fees, accounting costs, and administrative expenses. If there are claims against the estate, or any unpaid debts of the decedent, an executor must oversee and settle said matters.

The duties of an executor are **not ceremonial** or figurehead in purpose. Clear and specific tasks must be performed. To undertake these tasks, one's executor is granted certain legal authority for a limited span of time: usually 9 to 18 months.

Too often, the role importance of an executor is misunderstood. The will-appointed person rushes off to an attorney, and dumps everything into the attorney's lap. This is a shirking of duty. It is also a gross error in judgment and a costly mistake.

It is a mistake because attorneys are beholden to the legal system in which they practice, rather than to the personal desires and intentions of the decedent. Because so, most of the tax, accounting, and ministerial functions are farmed out to nonattorney professionals. Inevitably, the result is excessive legal fees and protracted delays in settling an estate.

The truth is that, except for quite complex estates and those involving will contests and recalcitrant debtors, an executor does not have to employ an attorney whatsoever! Even where "mini-probate" is required, a self-reliant executor can process said matters without an attorney. An executor has the legal power to do so. This book will tell you how. But we will also caution you as to those situations where an attorney is truly required.

Probably the most important duty of an executor is to prepare **Form 706: U.S. Death Tax Return**. This return has to be filed when a decedent's gross estate exceeds prescribed statutory amounts. An executor, under penalties of perjury, has to certify that Form 706 is . . . *true, correct, and complete.*

In general, Form 706 is required when a decedent's gross estate exceeeds $600,000. The term "gross estate" includes all property (real and personal), money, and financial accounts in which the decedent had an ownership interest . . . when **valued at date of death**. This includes insurance on the life of the decedent, survivor pensions and annuities, transfers during life without adequate consideration, powers of appointment (to someone else's estate), joint tenancies, community property, and dower or curtesy interests (in noncommunity states). Any property or accounts which are located outside of the United States, and subject to control and discretion by the decedent, are also included. Determining a decedent's gross estate is indeed a considerable undertaking. It requires a detailed inventory, backed up with documents and appraisals.

Even if the gross estate is less than $600,000, an executor must still list and value all assets and interests left by the decedent. This is necessary to prove that no Form 706 is required.

Regardless of whether Form 706 is required or not, an executor must prepare and file the decedent's "final" income tax return (**Form 1040**), and initiate a fiduciary income tax return (**Form 1041**). The fiduciary return begins on the day after date of death, and continues until the estate is settle. Sound contingency planning is required for properly closing the fiduciary estate. We have some unique suggestions for you in this regard.

Obviously, a deceased person cannot act as his/her own executor. Someone else must account for and distribute the residual estate, after the owner thereof dies. Doing so prudently and responsibly is the function of an executor. For his/her effort, an executor is entitled to reimbursement from the estate for out-of-pocket expenses . . . **and** a *compensatory fee*. Typically, this fee is approximately 2% of the decedent's gross estate.

On the subject of executor duties, this book covers many facets that you simply will not find elsewhere.

CONTENTS

1

FIRST THINGS FIRST

Every Testator Is Well Advised To Furnish His Executor A Copy Of His Will. This Makes Clear His Testamentary Choice Of A Personal Representative After Death. During Funeral, Burial, And Family Gathering Activities, The Duties Of An Executor Are Low Key And In The Background. It Is Not Until A "Certificate Of Death" Is Completed That One's Executorial Role Emerges. At This Point, The Will Copy Is Read By The Executor. Thereupon, He/She Sets Up A 9-Month Work Calendar For Accomplishment Of Specific Tasks.

A will is an instrument prepared in writing by an individual who wants his/her intentions made known, concerning disposition of property after death. Until actual death of the will-writer occurs, the instrument has no force or effect. It is an instrument-in-limbo; it can be changed any time, many times.

The person who writes a will is called the *testator*. As such, he/she has certain testamentary rights and privileges. These rights are inherent to human beings. They are embodied in The Preamble to the U.S. Constitution: "We the people . . . to secure the blessings of liberty to ourselves and our posterity (do) . . . ."

One of the testator's rights is to name and appoint in his will one or more persons to be his Executor/Executrix. Usually, at least two persons are so named. If so, one is the primary executor and the other is the ancillary executor. Sometimes a third or fourth executor is named as successor to the first named.

Thus, the very first duty of an executor is to find out if he/she has been named in someone's will.

How Appointment Known

Whenever one writes a will, he has to consciously think — and weigh the capabilities of — one or more persons to be his executor. Having done this, he then has to name and list the nominees in the order of succession of their appointments. This he must do in a separate paragraph known as the *executor nomination* paragraph.

A well-prepared will is written in a series of separately stated paragraphs, each paragraph being a self-contained subject of its own. This establishes clarity and conciseness, which are the essence of testamentary power and knowledge. Typically, an executor nomination paragraph might read as:

FOURTH
(or some other paragraph number)

I hereby nominate and appoint my wife, MARY JANE JONES, as Executrix of this my Last Will and Testament, and direct that she shall be empowered to act as such without bond. In the event that my wife should predecease me or for any reason be unable to act or continue as my Executrix, then I nominate and appoint my son, DAVID MARK JONES, as Executor to likewise act without bond. In the further event that my son should predecease me or for any reason be unable to act or continue as my Executor, then I nominate and appoint my brother-in-law, GARY CONRAD MORGAN, as Executor to likewise act without bond.

Once a testator has made his appointment in writing, the normal tendency is to notify in some manner those who have been so named. Rarely is a testator going to appoint an executor in his will without ever notifying the person (or persons) involved. There is nothing to be gained — and much to be lost — by "surprising" an executor after the testator's death.

The best way to make an appointment known is for the testator to give his primary appointee a copy of his will. Prudence suggests that this be a legally valid copy. We'll explain why in a moment.

For privacy reasons, the copy should be placed in a sealed envelope with bold-lettered captions thereon:

LAST WILL AND TESTAMENT
OF
JOHN QUINCY JONES

[Incidentally, all names herein are purely fictitious and are strictly for illustration purposes.]

Any executor should be mature enough to know that when handed a copy of someone's will, he does not open the envelope to read it. This is ordinary courtesy, even among close family members. The executor puts the sealed envelope away in a safe place for easy retrieval . . . if/when death of the testator indeed occurs.

"Conformed" Copy Advantageous

For prompt commencement of after-death duties, the copy of a will handed to an executor should be a *conformed* copy. That is, it should be an exact duplicate of the original will, together with full original signatures of the testator and witnesses. In this way, the original and conformed copy are interchangeable.

Why a conformed copy?

Because, in most cases, the testator or the attorney preparing the will takes the original and hides it away in a safe-deposit box, or in a padlocked file cabinet. This is done entirely unbeknown to the executor. When the testator dies, the executor is left in the dark as to the whereabouts of the original will.

If an attorney prepares the will and keeps the original, the executor often does not know who the attorney is, nor where he is. Attorneys can move from one place of business to another; they can consolidate their files with partners and associates; they can change their professional interests; and . . . they, too, can die. Even if an executor can locate the custodial attorney of a decedent's will, many attorneys resent and resist handing over the original will to an executor.

If a testator prepares his own will, as many do these days, he is unknowledgeable in what to do with the original. Too often, he secretes it away as though it were a negotiable pot of gold. He will not tell anyone where it is. He is so afraid that it will be stolen.

The greatest risks to the safe-keeping of a will are fire, flood, hurricane, tornado, or earthquake: *not* theft. A will is an absolutely worthless instrument while the testator is alive. No one is knowingly going to steal someone's will. Being a paper instrument, it can be destroyed by fire and natural disasters. Consequently, it makes good sense to prepare *two* original wills: the actual original and a conformed copy. If either of the two is lost or destroyed, the other serves equally as well.

With two original wills, the best safe-keeping action is to place them in two separate personal residences. One residence should be that of the testator; the other residence should be that of the executor. Ideally, the two residences should be so physically separated that a common fire or disaster is unlikely.

By keeping the two wills in two separate personal residences, they are accessible at all hours of the day/night, and all days/nights of the week. This ready accessibility does not exist if only one original will is locked up in an attorney's office or in a safe-deposit box at a financial institution.

The safe-keeping of a will sometimes presents a dilemma to testators and executors. But a little common sense is all that is needed. There are simple alternatives, which are depicted in Figure 1.1. The key to safe-keeping is *two* wills: one testator-retained and the other executor-retained.

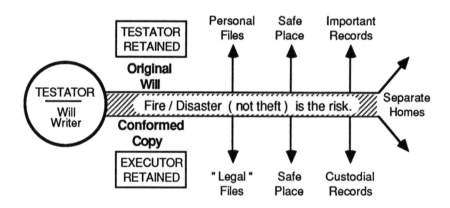

Fig. 1.1 - Alternative Safe-Keeping of Testator's Will

Problems With Co-Executors

Some testators, at the prodding of well-intentioned family members and close friends, designate all of their executor nominees as co-executors. As you probably know, the term "co" means . . .

equal, together, jointly. That is, all co-executors must act in unison. This is cumbersome and impractical. It can create unintentional problems.

Consider the three executors named in the foregoing paragraphic example: wife, son, and brother-in-law. Assume that they had been named co-executors, instead of successor executors as in the example. No matter how well these three persons may get along with each other while the testator is alive, and no matter how well they respect the wishes of the testator, when the testator dies, said three minds would rarely act as one. Chances are, they would be in different places at different times when some important decision is required. Three separate minds invariably interpret needs and events differently. And each one is intimidated differently by legal processes, accounting practices, tax forms, and other documents they are required to sign. Getting three signatures in order to undertake every executorial task raises many conflicts of interest.

When two or more co-executors are involved in the affairs of a decedent, more often than not antagonisms and contrary opinions grow. When this happens, a will contest is virtually guaranteed. This means probate court proceedings, the employment of attorneys (one for each co-executor), and endless haggling.

If the co-executors truly respect the wishes of the testator who appointed them, they should agree among themselves to eliminate all but one. The logical way to do this is to eliminate those who have a direct financial interest in the estate. A "financial interest" means the person or persons who ultimately will become owner/owners of the distributed estate. In the wife, son, and brother-in-law example above, the wife and son most likely would be the principal financial interests. Chances are, the brother-in-law would get none of the testator's estate. Therefore, he has no direct financial interest and is more likely than not to carry out his duties impartially.

It is rather obvious that the brother-in-law was appointed for his executorial capabilities, and that the wife and son were co-appointed for ceremonial reasons (not to hurt their feelings). In this case, the wife and son should defer to the brother-in-law, and eliminate themselves voluntarily. Do not worry; there are state laws which protect the financial interests of the wife and son from any abuses of discretion by the brother-in-law.

The elimination of a co-executor should be done in writing. It should be a specific renunciation/resignation from all executorial duties. Each renunciation should be an attachment to the will which is in the hands of the sole executor.

During the administrative/distributive phase of an estate, a sole executor does not "own" the assets thereof. He/she is simply the *accounting manager* of the estate. The testator is still the owner. He continues to be the owner, even in death, until the estate is finally settled by distribution to the new owner(s). We all know that solo management of the affairs of another is more efficient. It makes things go more smoothly and expeditiously.

Limit Your Predeath Queries

Knowing in advance that you are the sole executor of the estate of another does not mean that you should sit on your hands and wait. There are important inquiries that you should make to the testator before his/her actual death.

As executor, you are the person in whom the testator has full faith and trust. Most certainly, therefore, you and the testator should communicate with each other. In the communicative process, the testator will probably discuss with you some of the matters in the will. If the testator does this voluntarily, fine. But as executor, you should not press the testator to expound on the provisions of his will. The will will speak for itself . . . when death comes.

Nevertheless, you are not out of line by asking the testator who are the beneficiaries (distributees) of his estate, and where they are living. As opportunity permits, you should get full names, complete addresses, and current phone numbers. This is just prudent predeath preparation.

How much of the estate, and in what form, goes to each distributee is another matter. That is a decision for the testator alone to make. You should not invade his privacy by such direct or subtle inquiries. As an executor, you need not — should not — know these decisions ahead of time. Besides, a testator always has the right to change his mind without consultation with his executor.

It is not out of order for you to make inquiry as to the general location of important papers and records. This includes the whereabouts of insurance policies, title deeds, stock certificates, tax returns, and so on. Not specifics: but just enough information to become aware of the record-keeping habits of the testator. It is tragic the number of important estate papers that cannot be found until long after a testator deceases . . . if ever found at all.

Certainly, you should solicit some expressions of preference regarding the funeral and burial plans of the testator. In most cases, close family members (who are not executors) will do the final resting place arranging. But an executor should have some idea. This enables one to be mentally prepared to ask the right estate-accounting questions later.

All funeral /burial or cremation/memorial expenses from date of death to date of final resting, including the family gathering activities thereafter, are deductible from the decedent's gross estate. We will explain these matters more fully as we go along. In the meantime, we merely want to tip you off that recordation of funeral/burial and cremation/memorial expenses does come within the province of your executor duties.

When Death Occurs

When a testator dies, close family members, close relatives, and close friends are the first to know. This is because these persons usually keep in personal touch with the testator on a day-to-day, and sometimes hour-to-hour, basis. Unless you, as executor, are yourself a "close person" to the testator, you may not know first-hand when death occurs. It is not important that you do know first-hand. You will know later, in due course.

When death occurs to a loved one or close friend, human nature and emotion take over. There are expressions of sympathy and grievance. A communication "grape vine" springs up, and those who should be informed are informed. There is always someone around who knows what to do. Instinctively, first things come first. At this point, executor duties are completely irrelevant.

The very first notification of death should be made to the family doctor, if any; otherwise to a "duty physician" on call. Nothing can be done to the body of a deceased testator until a licensed physician examines said body and confirms the death. It cannot be moved, clothed, or whatever. The priority purpose of the examination is to rule out foul play, and get vital statistics for recordation in public records. An official *Certificate of Death* has to be prepared.

The initiation of a death certificate is outside of the duties of an executor or other persons close to the decedent. It is the attending physician who legally initiates the death certificate. He does this by entering the cause of death thereon: the immediate cause and the preceding conditions (if any) leading to the cause of death. The condition of the body, the date of death, and approximate hour also are noted by the physician. The physician has to personally sign the certificate and enter his license number.

Other details beyond those directly observable by the examining physician also are required on the death certificate. Such information is pulled together later from family and friends by county health officials and/or by the funeral director. Such information as date of birth, occupation, last residence, name of mortuary or funeral home, name of cemetery or crematorium, date/hour of burial, and so on.

In highly edited form, the general contents of a death certificate are presented in Figure 1.2. The information therein is for familiarization purposes only. As an executor, you have no responsibility for preparing the certificate. You should be aware that it is "in process," and you should know — or find out — whom to contact later for certified copies.

A "Funeral Observer" Only

Every moment from time of death through final burial (or cremation) is highly charged with emotion and sanctimony. All of the finest moral and religious tones of human beings come to the fore. Consequently, in such a setting, nothing is more devastating to holy spirits than an overreactive executor. The mature executor, who truly respects and regrets the death of his appointer, knows what to do. He stays in the background and he stays low key.

During the burial preparations and funeral activities, your function as an executor is purely an *observer*: no more, no less. You subordinate all of your executorial tasks entirely to the wishes and whims of close family members and friends. Until a deceased body is buried (or cremated) and the funeral/memorial activities are closed, you officially are a nonperson. So, stay in the background and observe.

In your observational role, however, do use your eyes and ears. Look, listen, and be present at all activities to which you are invited. For those activities to which you may not be invited, you may ask questions. But use discretion and tact. As an observer, you merely want to be aware of what's going on, and who is doing what. You do not want to interfere.

In your observational role, you should touch base with two specific persons: the burial (or cremation) coordinator and the funeral (or memorial) director.

The *burial coordinator* is a close family member who has taken on the chores of making key decisions concerning preparation and disposition of the testator's body. This includes such decisions as

---

CERTIFICATE OF DEATH , State of _____

FULL NAME OF DECEDENT		Date of Death:
Place of Death	Soc. Sec. No.	Hour:
Citizenship	Occupation	Age: Ethnicity: Sex: Race:
Last Residence: Street ; City ; County		Date of Birth: Birthplace:
Informant's Name / Address / Relationship		Marital Status:

CAUSE(S) OF DEATH

1. Immediate Cause _____
2. As a Consequence of _____
3. Other Condition Contributing _____
4. Related Operation Performed _____
5. Interval Between Onset and Death _____

Coroner informed?   Biopsy performed?   Autopsy performed?

CERTIFICATION BY PHYSICIAN
Date ; Name ; Address ; License No. ; Last Attended ; Signature

CERTIFICATION BY CORONER
Nature of Death (Accident / Suicide) ; Inquest / Investigation

PLACE OF BURIAL / CREMATION
Month, Day, Year ; Name / Address of Cemetery / Crematory
Name of Mortuary / Funeral Director / Embalmer (License No.)

ACCEPTANCE BY LOCAL REGISTRAR
Name / Signature / Date ; District No. ; Certificate No. _____

Fig. 1.2 - General Contents of a Death Certificate

embalming, cremation, burial attire, type of casket, type of urn, use of flowers, date and hour of burial or cremation, nomenclature on headstone or plaque, menu for the family gathering, and many other related chores, including seating/standing arrangements of family, relatives, and guests. The burial coordinator has many decisions to make in a short span of time: 3 to 5 days at most. Everyone associated with the decedent must cooperate unselfishly. The burial coordinator performs out of pure love and respect for the decedent.

The *funeral director* is a paid professional. He is an employee of a mortuary, funeral home, crematorium, or cemetery. He visits the unprepared situs of the body, and engages all of the necessary talent and facilities for carrying out the decisions of the burial coordinator. He obtains information for publishing the obituary, and for completing the death certificate. He keeps track of all costs associated with funeral/memorial services for which he is responsible. As executor, you will need to know these costs later. You will need also to know about other costs.

Circulate at Family Gathering

Following the funeral/memorial services in respect of a decedent, it is common practice to have a family gathering. Family, friends, and compassionates get together to eat in a congenial atmosphere honoring the deceased, and recalling those precious moments of the past. Quite often, some guests have come from long distances and want to "flash back" into memory lane.

If, as executor, you have shared memories with guests — and even if not — the family gathering is an opportunity to build a rapport with those associates close to the decedent. You should make mental notes on who they are (name, address, occupation) and the extent of their relations with the deceased. Do this by circulating among the guests as unobtrusively as possible. Be understanding and tactful. If someone asks about your interests, answer them. But do not openly advertise your executorial duties.

However, you can come out of the background a little bit. It is your chance to get acquainted with those associates of the decedent whom you may have to contact later by phone or mail. At this point, you have no knowledge of what is in the decedent's will (other than that you are his/her appointed executor). Consequently, you are not in a position to seek specific information from the decedent's associates. Just keep in mind that any and all social, business, financial, family, and other relations may become important to you later.

After all funeral/memorial guests have departed, and after burial/cremation is a recorded statistic, you are now at liberty to open the envelope containing the decedent's will. You may do this initially in your own privacy, or in the presence of close family members.

Read Names of Distributees

By reading the will to close family members, you — and the decedent — are acquainting them with the fact that you are the appointed executor. The distributees need to know this. Whether you read the conformed copy or the actual original is irrelevant. You want to read it carefully — and reread it as necessary — to make sure that the decedent's intentions are clearly understood by those in attendance.

From your reading of the will, particularly note the names of the distributees. "Distributees" are those persons and entities who are to ultimately receive the decedent's distributable estate. Write down their names, their relationship to the decedent, their beneficial share of the estate, and their specifically bequested assets, if any.

There could be as few as one distributee . . . or as many as ten (or more). The number of distributees is strictly within the testamentary province of the decedent. Purely as an instructional example, consider that there are six distributees, as follows:

(1) Mary Jane Jones, surviving spouse
   — marital residence plus all residual estate after the bequests below
(2) David Mark Jones, oldest child (adult)
   — $150,000 or its equivalent in value
(3) Jane Elizabeth Jones, youngest child (minor)
   — $350,000 or 35% of residual estate, whichever is higher
(4) Thomas King Elder, close business associate
   — all shares of the U-Know-What Mutual Fund
(5) Trinity Alps Church
   — that parcel of land located in Trinity County
   — all personal belongings and effects unwanted by heirs
(6) Prudhoe Nautical Museum
   — all maritime books, alumni records, and nautical artifacts

As executor, you have legal obligation to all of the decedent's distributees. Note who they are and where they are. You may contact them informally. In due time, however, you will have to notify them formally. Also, in due time, you will have to give each one a "final accounting" of the distributable estate. One or more of the distributees could become your adversary, if you are slipshod and negligent in your executorial duties.

You might also consider other potential adversaries, whether named in the will or not. For example, an ex-spouse; a "passed over" child; a "promised" nephew; a disgruntled business associate; and others. These persons generally "come out of the woodwork" when they learn of the decedent's death. If they do, take care to record their names and their claims. They can make real trouble for you by hiring attorneys to contest the will.

Start 9-Month Calendar

When you are through reading this book, you will know what we mean when we say that there are many executorial tasks to perform. We are warming up to them now. You are not expected to accomplish all of the tasks overnight. You could not do so, even if you wanted to. There are too many persons, entities, assets, and procedures involved.

Unless you have been an executor before, you'll have an entirely new experience in life. It is unlike any other single task that you have performed. You will make some mistakes. So, do not fret and stew. We will take you step-by-step (chapter by chapter) through your executorial experience.

At this point, Step 1 in the executorial process is to open the envelope containing the will (after burial/cremation and the family gathering). Read and reread as necessary to comprehend the testator's wishes. List all of the distributees and those who might claim to be such. Do not contact them yet. Just be aware who they are. List the property item(s) each is to receive.

Step 2 is to "start your calendar" . . . and pace yourself. Set your final goal to complete all estate affairs within nine months of the decedent's death. If you proceed persistently and diligently, you *can* complete the process within nine months.

Why do we pick nine months?

Because Section 6075(a) of the Internal Revenue Code reads:

Returns . . . (relating to estate taxes) shall be filed within 9 months after the date of the decedent's death.

Your task now is to start a nine-month calendar of activities, and work diligently within that time frame. Set specific goals for accomplishment each month. You don't have to work every minute of every day on estate affairs, but you do have to think ahead and seek specific accomplishments. To assist you in this regard, we present Figure 1.3.

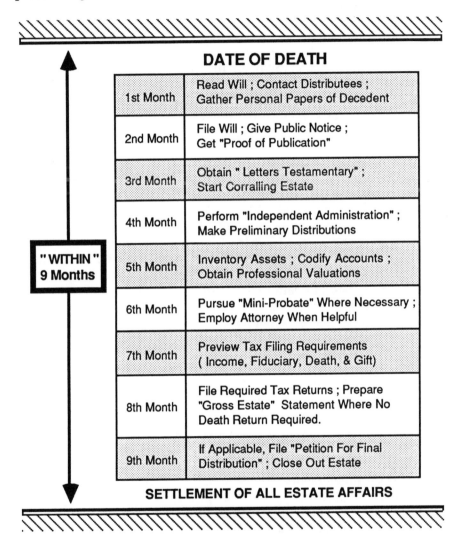

DATE OF DEATH

1st Month	Read Will ; Contact Distributees ; Gather Personal Papers of Decedent
2nd Month	File Will ; Give Public Notice ; Get "Proof of Publication"
3rd Month	Obtain " Letters Testamentary" ; Start Corralling Estate
4th Month	Perform "Independent Administration" ; Make Preliminary Distributions
5th Month	Inventory Assets ; Codify Accounts ; Obtain Professional Valuations
6th Month	Pursue "Mini-Probate" Where Necessary ; Employ Attorney When Helpful
7th Month	Preview Tax Filing Requirements (Income, Fiduciary, Death, & Gift)
8th Month	File Required Tax Returns ; Prepare "Gross Estate" Statement Where No Death Return Required.
9th Month	If Applicable, File "Petition For Final Distribution" ; Close Out Estate

" WITHIN "
9 Months

SETTLEMENT OF ALL ESTATE AFFAIRS

Fig. 1.3 - Time Calendar for Your Executorial Duties

Figure 1.3 depicts the major highlights of your duties. These highlights introduce you to various points of progress that you are expected to accomplish. As you should suspect, there are many subordinate details of preparation and pursuit. Treat each monthly goal-point as a learning experience. You have ample time so do not rush, and do not panic. Above all . . . do not procrastinate.

Beware of "Stalking"

To *stalk* someone is to pursue that person (you) mercilessly as a victim of prey. The stalker watches every move — every little detail — in the hope that the person stalked will stumble, incur a defect, or be caught off-guard. At the opportune moment, the stalker pounces. The purpose of his/her pouncing is to have you removed as executor of the estate.

The most likely stalkers are heirs, legatees, and their counsel. Heirs are family members and relatives, whereas legatees are friends, associates, and organizations who have been named in the will as beneficiaries. Their "counsel" is usually some attorney who has been made aware of your being will-appointed as executor, and who is smarting under his/her skin that you have not engaged him/her as attorney for the estate. As you will see in the next chapter, you have all of the powers of any attorney during the period of time from date of death to date of final distribution of the estate. But if you fail in some material way to perform your legal duties, you can be removed as executor.

Unfortunately, you may be stalked simply because some heir or legatee fails to understand the necessity for the procedures in Figure 1.3, and accuses you of deliberately dragging things out. The accuser becomes impatient with the holdup in getting his/her share of the estate and, as a result of this impatience, may engage an attorney to have you removed.

You can protect yourself against being removed as executor. The best way to do this is to establish a *statutory schedule*. This would be in addition to your general work schedule in Figure 1.3. A statutory schedule would list specific dates when certain legal duties must be performed. These dates are prescribed in the probate code of the state where the deceased died. We'll discuss these dates in subsequent chapters, as we go along.

2

MUST TAKE CHARGE

Your First "Take Charge" Action Is To Locate And
Retrieve The Original Will. To Gain Confidence In
Doing So, Visit Your Public Library And Skim Through
The Probate Code For Your State. Particularly Note—
And Photocopy—Your Executorial Powers. Then Prepare
Your "Initial" Statutory Calendar, And Start Keeping
Records. Keep Always In Focus Your Primary Role:
That Of A Short-Term Manager-Accountant. As A
Nonfigurehead, You Are Entitled To Reimbursement For
Expenses And A Fee For Services.

Following the burial/cremation of a deceased testator, there
usually is a short period of mourning. This is a natural aftermath
where the decedent has touched the hearts and souls of close
persons. A dutiful executor, therefore, must respect the rights of
those truly in mourning.

Typically, a period of mourning lasts from a few days to a few
weeks. Rarely should it last more than a month after death. Other
lives — and other matters — must go on. As executor, you must
come to the fore and make your presence and appointment known.

All too often, nonprofessional executors tend to flounder
around. They procrastinate . . . and procrastinate because they are
not sure of what to do. They talk to friends, neighbors, and
associates, trying to get pointers and direction. Instead, they get
misinformation and misdirection. So, they flounder some more.

Instead of floundering, you must "take charge" and get going.
Although you have nine months to accomplish your tasks, you must

not stand aside for eight months before taking charge. At no more than 30 days after death, you must overtly assume your duties and get going. You really must.

Retrieve the Original Will

Your very first "take charge" effort is to locate and retrieve the original will. It is true that you may have the conformed copy, but it is not the original. The original is prima facie evidence of your appointment and authority. You have a legal obligation to either locate and retrieve the original, or declare under oath that it cannot be located. There can be only one original.

Chances are, the original can be found in one of three probable locations. It may be among the personal papers and effects of the decedent at his last residence. Or, it may be in a safe-deposit box at his favorite bank or savings institution. Or, it may be in the possession of an attorney whom the decedent last contacted before death. Wherever it is, you must find it. When you do, you must take physical possession of it.

If a will is located on the last premises of the decedent, there is usually no retrieval problem. You simply find it and take possession of it. Most family members and custodians of the decedent's personal effects understand that a will belongs to the executor who is to administer and execute it.

Sometimes, actually, finding a will among the personal effects of a decedent is awkward. One has to rummage through files and clutter and sort of stumble on it. Rarely does a testator have his papers and files so well organized that his will pops out on the first search. Often it is not clearly identified as such. Thus, an executor has to glance-read several will-looking papers to be sure that one is indeed the testator's "Last Will and Testament."

Whatever is your success in this regard, do not destroy the conformed copy. It has all of the original signatures and therefore is a legal substitute. Keep the conformed copy in your own possession until, at least, the estate is final-settled.

Sticky Access to Safe-Deposit Boxes

Though not a good practice, many testators automatically lock their wills in a safe-deposit box at a local bank or savings institution. If this is the case, you as the executor first have to locate the safe-deposit box key. Usually, this is somewhere among the personal effects of the decedent.

Finding the safe-deposit box key and going to the local depository is a task unto itself. You can gain access to such box only when the depository institution is regularly open for business. This is one hurdle.

The next hurdle is to gain access to the safe-deposit box itself. If your signature for box entry is already on file with the depository institution, you have no particular problem. An officer of the institution will accompany you to the box and witness your removal of the will.

If your signature for box entry is not on file with the depository institution, you will experience many frustrations. Regardless of whether you are the executor or not, an officer of the institution will not permit your access without some other authorization. Showing him or her the conformed copy of the decedent's will, will *not* be impressive; it will not gain you access. "Other authorization" definitely will be required.

Among the authorizing alternatives for access to the safe-deposit box are:

1. Be accompanied by the surviving signatory joint tenant, if any;
2. Presentation of an Administrative Consent signed by the County Treasurer (or other local inheritance referee);
3. Obtain Letters Testamentary from the applicable probate court;
4. Obtain a specific Court Order to depository institution, directing access and removal of the will (and other related papers).

As you can see, access to a safe-deposit box by persons other than the decedent owner is a sticky procedure. And properly so. This is the reason why storing a will with a depository institution is not recommended.

Difficulties With Attorneys

Many testators, not knowing otherwise what to do, simply allow the attorney who prepared their will to retain it in his/her files. When this is done, most testators will prepare a list of persons to contact upon their demise. If the attorney's name is listed or otherwise becomes known to you, your duty is to contact that attorney and request that the original be forwarded to you. But be prepared for resistance and static.

Even though you are clearly the decedent's appointed executor, an attorney who is custodian of the will will quiz and cross-quiz you. You will be led to believe — yes, even intimidated — into thinking that only the attorney who prepared the will has the right to possess it. Many attorneys will not voluntarily release a will to someone who is a non-attorney.

If this should become your experience, you have a challenge that will test your mettle. Contact the bar association in the county where the attorney practices. State that you want to enter a complaint against the attorney possessing the will. Request local procedures thereon. You may be told to contact some ethics committee member (another attorney) of the bar association. If so, prepare a written complaint to the ethics committee, and send a copy to the resistive attorney. Chances are, said attorney still will not deliver the will to you.

Your next course is to request that the custodial attorney deliver the will to the clerk of the probate court having jurisdiction over the decedent. State law (the Probate Code) is on your side in this request. In California, for example, Section 8200 of its Probate Code states—

*The custodian of a will shall, within 30 days after having knowledge of the death of the testator, do both of the following: (1) Deliver the will to the clerk of the superior court of the county in which the estate of the decedent may be administered. (2) Mail a copy of the will **to the person named** in the will **as executor**.* [Emphasis added.]

Note the emphasized phrase above "to the person named . . . as executor." This is pretty clear evidence that you have legal authority to request any custodial attorney to deliver the will to you. So do not be intimidated by his/her resistance to do so.

Some custodial attorneys go so far as to never deliver the will to the executor. Instead, they will deliver it only to the probate clerk. Once so delivered, it becomes a public record. As the executor "named in the will," you have the right and duty to pay the clerk's fee and get a certified copy of the original. The original will itself is thereby surrendered into the legal system, whether probate is required or not.

Visit Your Public Library

The experience in retrieving the original will may raise doubt in your mind as to your legal powers and duties. The experience may also prompt you to seek more definitive knowledge in the executorial domain.

Knowledge is a wonderful commodity. With it you have the courage to complete the tasks expected of you. Without knowledge, you can be pushed around by professionals and others who want to take over your duties . . . and charge you a fee.

To bolster your confidence in your executor undertakings, we urge you to schedule a few hours to visit your public library (which has a law section). Ask the librarian for assistance in locating an up-to-date copy of the *probate code* of the state in which the decedent died. All states have a probate code which is available for reference at public locations.

All matters pertaining to decedent persons are addressed in the probate code of a given state. You do not have to be an attorney to look at the probate code in your public library. Anyone with some initiative can do so. Do not be intimidated by the word "probate." It simply means "to prove" or "to substantiate" something.

When you locate your library edition of the probate code, find a table nearby and sit down. Quickly skim through the pages, cover to cover, back and forth. Then look at the Table of Contents. Here and there read the page headings, the chapter titles, and the section subheadings. Make no attempt to read any parts in depth. The mere fact of actually holding the probate code in your hands is — in itself — a confidence-building factor. You now have at your fingertips all the pearls of statutory wisdom of all executors before you. Realizing this, the mystery, awe, and fear of the unknown should begin to fade.

Once you have skim-read the headings and subheadings, home in on that chapter (or division) titled "**Administration of Estates of Decedents**" or similar title. Mark the beginning and ending of that chapter with slips of paper. Then skim-read that chapter alone, making mental notes of those topics that appear to immediately affect you. As an example of the coverage you would find in such a chapter, we present Figure 2.1. Simply skim-reading this figure alone will give you some idea of what is covered in the probate code of a state like California.

Either from Figure 2.1 or from perusal of your own state's probate code, select no more than three topics applicable to you and

CALIFORNIA PROBATE CODE
Division 7
ADMINISTRATION OF ESTATES OF DECEDENTS

Part	Heading	Section
1.	General Provisions	7000
2.	Opening Estate Adminstration	8000
3.	Inventory and Appraisal	8800
4.	Creditor Claims	9000
5.	Estate Management	9600
6.	Independent Administration	10400
7.	Accounts and Records	10900
8.	Payment of Debts	11400
9.	Distribution of Estate	11600
10.	Closing Estate Administration	12200
11.	Estates of Missing Persons	12400
12.	Nondomiciliary Decedents	12500

OTHER DIVISIONS OF CALIFORNIA PROBATE CODE

Division 1.	Preliminary Provisions and Definitions
Division 2.	General Provisions and Powers
Division 3.	Provisions of a Procedural Nature
Division 4.	Guardianship and Conservatorship
Division 5.	Nonprobate Transfers
Division 6.	Wills and Intestate Succession
Division 7.	(LISTED ABOVE)
Division 8.	Dispositions Without Administration
Division 9.	Trust Law
Division 10.	Proration of Taxes
Division 11.	Construction of Wills and Trusts

Fig. 2.1 - Example Organization of a Probate Code

your decedent's estate. Then read these topics rather thoroughly. Do not read more than three topics. Otherwise, you'll become overwhelmed and discouraged.

One topic that you should definitely read, in whole or part, is "Estate Management." Subtopics would be such items as—

(1) Management and control of estate
(2) Powers and duties of executor
(3) Deposits and withdrawals of money

. . . and others of your choice. It is a good idea to make photocopies of the topics you have selected so that you can take them home. Most public libraries have copy machines available. So, have some coin change with you when you go to the library.

Study Your Executorial Powers

A couple of hours at your public library is all that you need to get an introductory familiarity with your role as an executor. After this, go home and read carefully the executor paragraphs in the decedent's will.

Most wills include a paragraph or two which delineate the powers and duties of the executor. Find these paragraphs and focus exclusively on them. Read—and reread—as you like. Note carefully certain words and phrases therein. You want to be sure that you have the testator's approval for those actions necessary to carry out his wishes.

A typical *executor powers* paragraph might read as follows:

FIFTH
(or other paragraph number)
I direct that my Executor or Executrix, whoever it may be, shall have full power to sell, exchange, or transfer as much of the property of my estate as he or she deems advisable, in order to distribute and settle my estate as directed herein, by independent administration, without giving notice, without judicial accounting, and without court supervision. I specifically direct that all debts, expenses, and taxes applicable to my estate be paid; that all assets be distributed; and that my estate be settled within nine (9) months of my demise.

A will assigning power to an executor with the above specificity is pretty clear. The testator means business. He does not want his executor to "fool around" with probate courts and probate attorneys. He wants his executor to do the job efficiently and expeditiously.

Even with such a clear-cut paragraph in the will, some executors are nervous and hesitant about their powers and authority. Somehow, they feel that a testator cannot grant them such power. They seek legal counsel.

Instead of seeking costly legal counsel, the best antidote to any nervousness is to go back to the public library. If you have not done so previously, photocopy the topical section on *Powers of Executor*. Some states like California have diluted these powers and segregated them into separate subsections under: **Powers and duties of personal representatives** (Sec. 9650). Then, based on a prior section (namely: Sec. 8420), its probate code says—

The person named as executor in the decedent's will has the right to appointment as personal representative. . . . The personal representative has the right to, and shall take possession or control of, all of the estate of the decedent . . . and shall collect all debts due to the decedent or to the estate. [He/she] is entitled to receive the rents, issues, and profits from the real and personal property in the estate until the estate is settled or delivered . . . to the heirs and devisees. [He/she] shall pay taxes on, and take all steps reasonably necessary for the management, protection, and preservation of, the estate [while] in his or her possession.

The California probate code then goes on to detail other specific powers and duties of an executor, such as—

- Deposit of money and personal property (Sec. 9700)
- Investments and purchase of property (Sec. 9730)
- Operation of decedent's business (Sec. 9760)
- Abandonment of tangible personal items (Sec. 9780)
- Borrowing, refinancing, and encumbering property (Sec. 9800)
- Dedication or conveyance to government (Sec. 9900)
- Exchanges and leases of property (Sec. 9920)
- Sale of property to pay debts, etc. (Sec. 10000)

With statutory references like the above, what possible additional authority or guidance do you need? It's all there in the probate code of your state.

Once you find the executor duties and powers in your state's probate code, it's a good idea to photocopy them and keep them in your files. A better idea is to note the name and address of the publisher of the probate code, then write or phone for a "compact edition." The cost would run between $25 and $50 . . . payable out of the estate. This would save visiting your public library more than once.

Note Key "Statutory Dates"

Your powers as executor do not go on indefinitely. Consequently, you must knuckle down and start your statutory calendar as to what must be done when. Note that we say "start" your calendar; this does not mean that you have to prepare a detailed listing of all legal events for the entire nine months of your tenure. Simply look ahead to the first three or four months.

Statutory dates are usually indicated in the probate code with such phrases as *"within _____ days after"* . . . some prescribed event. You can find these phrases by browsing through such chapters as: "Opening Estate Administration," "Inventory and Appraisal," "Creditor Claims," etc. in the probate code of your state. Look for the subsections on: Time of Commencement, Notice of Hearing, Publication of Notice, Filing of Inventory, Filing of Claims, etc. Now do you see why we urge that you purchase a compact (paperback) edition of your state's probate code? You can note and flag these statutory dates sequentially.

For example, earlier we quoted a section requiring the will to be filed with the probate clerk of the court of jurisdiction. The opening phrase in that section says —

*The custodian of a will shall, **within 30 days after** having knowledge of the death of the testator . . .*

Take care to note that "within 30 days" does not mean within 30 days after death. It means 30 days after the custodian of the original will is notified of the death. So, take whatever time is necessary to read the full content of each statutory duty that you have to perform.

Another point to note is that statutory dates are not fixed in concrete. As long as reasonable cause can be shown, any date can be extended for a reasonable period of time.

Your initial statutory calendar should focus on that point in time when you have the estate fully inventoried, and all creditor claims (debts, taxes, and expenses) identified. At such point, you should have a fairly good handle on estate affairs. You'll then feel comfortable and confident when dealing with the beneficiaries of the will (and their counselors). It is doubtful that you can reach this stage in less than four months after date of death.

Figure 2.2 is intended to give you a little guidance for your initial calendaring. The items indicated are the key ones that you should be looking for when browsing the probate code. You might also check the key dates with the probate clerk where the will is to be filed.

10 Copies of Death Certificate

The statutory dates in Figure 2.2 are indicative of certain procedural steps that should be taken in sequence, whether you go to probate or not. In preparing for this "legal sequence," you will need certain documents. Foremost, of course, is proof of death.

Your best proof of death document is the Death Certificate. (Recall Figure 1.2.) You will need numerous copies of this document. Certainly, you will need one copy (certified) for your own records. And you'll need many others. Insurance agents, employers, social security administration (if applicable), title companies, tax returns, and a host of other bank, business, and financial institutions need some form of "proof" of death.

There are two ways of getting certified copies of the death certificate. The simplest way is to contact the funeral director employed on behalf of the decedent. Doing this by phone is so easy. Request the number of copies that you want, and they will be mailed to you in a few days. Most funeral homes keep reproducible copies of death certificates for their own business records. They reproduce your requested number of certificates and dispatch a courier to the county health department for the certifications. For their services, they charge a nominal fee.

The second way is for you yourself to visit the county health department, Registrar of Vital Statistics. Of course, you have to first identify the decedent's full name and date of death. Then you have to prepay the certification fee (at about $5 to $10 per copy). A

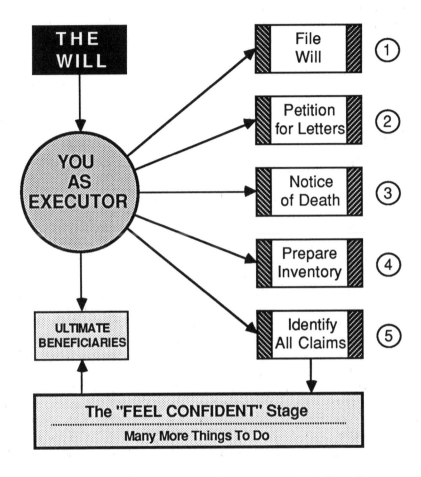

Fig. 2.2 - Initial Milestones of Executor "Statutory Dates"

week or two later, you will receive the certified copies in the mail. Due to delays in microfilm access and other clerk routines, it is doubtful that you could walk away from the county office with certificates in hand.

There will be times when you "want-now" a certified death certificate for some important task. You may not be able to tolerate the waiting period following your request(s). Rather than risk this inconvenience, it is advisable to order ample copies of death certificates in advance. A suggested number is 10 copies. They are relatively cheap and being a single sheet are easy to store in an envelope. Even if 10 copies seem excessive to you at this moment, you never know when unforeseen needs will pop up.

Quite often, when the funeral director learns of your capacity as executor, he will ask you early on the number of copies you want. He may do this at the time he prepares the obituary information. If he does so, do not equivocate. Without any explanation to him, cite the figure 10. He knows that ultimately you will need ample copies, whatever the number may be.

Open Estate Checking Account

Your next specific take-charge action is to open an estate checking account. You must do this without delay.

Go to a depository institution that is most convenient for you, and one that is easy to do business with. Of course, pick one where the deposits are federally insured. Get a checking-only account. Forget about any interest earnings, as you will probably be closing the account within nine months. You want a safe, convenient, and easy place to "park" money during your executor phase of activity.

For expeditious opening of such account, take with you your own personal check (or savings withdrawal) in the amount of, say, $100. You want to open the account in the name of the decedent and make an initial deposit without hassle.

If you go to a regulated depository institution with a check or other monetary instrument made payable to the decedent, you *will* be hassled. You will be asked to show your Letters Testamentary. (We will discuss this in Chapter 3.) Or, you will be told to get an attorney . . . and so on. Respond that you will apply for letters on your own.

Your objective is to open the account with minimum fuss. No depository institution will fuss if you put your own money in, even if it is in someone else's account. Do not worry; you will get it back from the estate later.

You open the account in the decedent's name, followed by your name as executor. For example, suppose the decedent's full name is John Quincy Jones, and your name is Gary Conrad Morgan. You open the account as follows:

Estate of John Quincy Jones, Deceased
Gary Conrad Morgan, Executor

Chances are, the depository institution will suggest some variant to this wording so as to fit into its own format. Always use the decedent's full name (no initials) unless it is obviously too awkward to do so. Initials sometimes lead to confusion with similar names in the roster of depository accounts. Your name and signature only should be on the authorization card for withdrawals. You should not dilute your responsibility with alternatively authorized signatures.

Once the account is opened — but not on the same day — deposit any and all monetary instruments made payable to the decedent, in the estate account. You do this by endorsing said instrument(s) as—

For Deposit to the
Estate of John Quincy Jones, Deceased
Gary Conrad Morgan, Executor

From this point on, there should be no hassle. Most depository institutions will accept monetary instruments for deposit, regardless of to whom they are made payable, so long as an account is opened and an authorized signature withdrawal card is on file.

Be sure to order a commercial-type check book with large-size stubs. Pay whatever fee is necessary. Don't haggle over the fee, or over the color, or over the imprinting. You want the largest stub size in their inventory. Preferably you want stubs with two or more lines prefaced with "For." You want ample room to write in an accurate explanation of each withdrawal. Somewhere along the line, some disgruntled distributee, agency, entity, or professional person may accuse you of mishandling the estate funds. If such accusations should arise, well-annotated check stubs will stand in your defense.

Focus on Your Primary Function

As you have probably surmised by now, you will have to account for all deposits into and expenditures from the estate checking account. The reason is that you have a very unusual job. The primary function of your job is to corral all assets of the estate and convert them into liquid (depository) form as much as practicable. You have to pay all taxes, claims, debts, and expenses. And, finally, you will have to distribute the remaining deposits and undeposited assets to the new owners designated in the will.

Not every executor fully comprehends his/her primary role. They engage in false starts and debilitating distractions. They lose sight entirely of their key function and purpose. An executor is a *short-term manager-accountant* only; he is not an entrepreneur. Nor is he second fiddle to some professional whiz.

To assist you in better understanding of your primary focus, Figure 2.3 is presented. It is a summary overview only. We will expand on the pertinent details in subsequent chapters. In the meantime, visualize yourself as the sole custodian of the estate checking account in Figure 2.3. Everything of the decedent — his assets *and* his liabilities — must pass through your hands. For a limited span of time, you are the hub of all accounting activities.

With Figure 2.3 in mind, it should be apparent that you must set up some sort of itemized/codified system of accounts. Do so in a manner that is simple and easy for yourself. Don't try to overdo. Don't try to become an accounting expert. Even though you have the authority to invest estate money, and borrow against estate assets, we urge you to forego these activities. Stick to your main

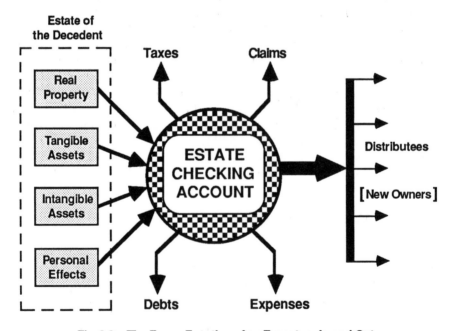

Fig. 2.3 - The Focus Function of an Executor : In and Out

accounting role. Your objective is to get everything INTO and OUT OF the estate checking account as quickly and as efficiently as possible.

The Matter of Executor Fee

By now you should recognize that you are not a figurehead functionary. You have real tasks to perform. You have duties and responsibilities. You will be manager-accountant of an estate worth, perhaps, $500,000 to $3,000,000 (3 million) dollars, or possibly more. For this responsibility, you are entitled to compensation for your personal services.

Most states permit the executor to claim a fee against the estate of the decedent. The amount of fee awarded is a prescribed percentage of the gross value of the estate. It is actually a *commission* rather than an hourly fee rate. It is the same idea as commission compensation paid to real estate agents and stock brokers.

California, for example, treats executor compensation in five specific sections of its probate code. With the section headings edited for more direct clarity, they are—

Sec. 900   — *Allowance of expenses and compensation;*
Sec. 901   — *Commissions when not provided in will;*
Sec. 902   — *Additional compensation: extraordinary services;*
Sec. 903   — *Invalidity of contracts for higher compensation;*
Sec. 904   — *Allowance of commissions upon petition.*

In particular, Section 904 says, in part—

Any executor . . . at any time after four months from the issuance of letters testamentary . . . upon such notice to the persons interested in the estate . . . may petition . . . for an allowance upon his or her commissions.

Typically, the statutory commissions are 3% for estates up to $100,000; 2% for estates up to $3,000,000; and 1% for larger estates.

Whether you actually claim an executor commission or not depends on your own circumstances. It also depends on your relationship to the decedent. If you are the surviving spouse of the decedent, or the only child of a single decedent parent, there is no point in claiming the fee. You will inherit all the decedent's property without any tax to you. If you claim the fee, it not only reduces your inheritance, it subjects the fee to personal income tax: federal and state.

If you are not a named distributee in the will, by all means claim the statutory fee. Also claim reimbursement for all necessary expenses that you pay out of your own pocket, and claim additional fees for any *extraordinary services* that you perform. By the time you complete your duties and responsibilities, you will know that you have earned the money.

3

LETTERS TESTAMENTARY

For Estates Over $500,000, It Is Doubtful That You Can Do All Things Necessary Without Letters Testamentary. Obtaining "Letters" Involves Filing A Petition For Probate, Attaching The Will Thereto, And Publishing Notice Of Death In A General Area Newspaper. Thereafter, Proof Of Subscribing Witness(es), Acknowledgment By Named Noticees, Proof Of Publication, And Attendance At A Hearing Are Required. An "Order For Probate" Directs The Court Clerk To Issue You Letters. You Should Request At Least Three Copies Of "Certified Letters."

Letters testamentary. What's that!

In an unabridged dictionary, you will find that "letters testamentary" means:

A written instrument from a court or officer thereof informing an executor of his appointment and of his authority to execute the will of the decedent.

In layman language, letters testamentary are like a "power of attorney" after death. They are the legal right — court approved — to do whatever is necessary to carry out the intentions in the will.

Ordinarily, a power of attorney is useful only during the life of the grantor. For this reason, preprinted power-of-attorney forms can be obtained from office supply/stationery stores, and signed by the grantor in the presence of a notary. But letters testamentary cannot be so obtained. The instrument is authorized only by the probate court having jurisdiction where the decedent died, or where he had property.

Are letters testamentary necessary where the decedent expressly appointed his executor, with proper powers?

Technically, no. But practically, yes.

It is doubtful that you would be able to complete all of your executorial duties without letters testamentary. This is particularly so if you have a semi-complex estate. With "letters" you can do things much easier than without them.

The Practicality of Letters

As a "take charge" executor, it will be necessary for you to contact various persons and entities. Some of the contacts will be custodians of your decedent's property; some will be debtors to the decedent; some will be donees/transferees/appointees of the decedent; and some will be creditors to the decedent. Despite what we said in Chapter 2, some of the persons and entities that you contact simply will not respond. You have the authority . . . but, so what!

Custodians and debtors, particularly, like to taunt and "bait" you. They want to make you prove who you say you are. They want to demoralize and force you to get an attorney (which you don't need). While they are taunting and baiting, they continue in possession of your decedent's assets and they continue not paying their bills. This is not just a game; it provides them with definite monetary advantages. They gain the "free use" of your decedent's assets and money. The taunting stops when you furnish them a copy of your approved letters.

Another situation often arises. The decedent's property and/or his debtors and/or his transferees are located outside of the state where the decedent last resided. State laws are not uniform in recognizing the right of a testator (decedent) to appoint and empower his own executor. Consequently, when a custodian, debtor, or transferee is beyond the jurisdiction of the death state, each is uncomfortable in complying with your requests. Each wants to see some kind of judicial documentation on the matter. A photocopy of your letters usually suffices.

Within the death state, you could demand executorial rights . . . without letters. But you would have to supply a complete (certified) copy of the will, and a complete quotation of applicable sections of the probate code. This could well involve 10, 20, or more pages of documentation. Thus, for each executorial request, you would have to supply a mass of attachments, carefully indexed. If more than one or two requests are made, numerous supporting attachments can become quite impractical.

In contrast, letters testamentary comprise one sheet of paper . . . on one side only. It is a certified court order with the court's seal embossed thereon. It is so much easier to send a photocopy of your letters than multiple pages of attachments. It all boils down to being a simpler way of administering the estate.

There is only one problem with letters. Some formality of procedure is required before getting them. You have to apply to the probate court having jurisdiction. You have to prepare some legal papers and forms, and pay a filing/hearing fee. This takes a minimum of from 30 to 60 days.

No; you do not need to employ an attorney to get your letters. As a take-charge executor, you can — and should — obtain them yourself. Approach the matter as a learning experience. Who knows? Someday you may want to pass the experience on to your own executor.

Overview of Procedures

We are not going to leave you out on a limb for obtaining letters. We will give you general guidance. We want to caution you, however, that the procedures will differ from state to state, and from county to county within a given state.

First, there is the matter of which court has proper jurisdiction. Since "probate" means proving the will, jurisdiction rests with that superior court of the county having jurisdiction over the decedent's will. Typically, this county is where the decedent last resided; that is, his domicile. But, often, a person resides in one county, dies in another county (or state), and has property in still another county (or state). Which county has jurisdiction?

Where more than one county is involved in the affairs of a decedent, there is a priority of jurisdictions. There are four such priorities, namely:

Priority 1 The county where the decedent was a resident at the time of his death.

Priority 2 The county where the decedent died, having property therein, even though not a resident thereof.

Priority 3 The county where the decedent has his primary estate, even if not a resident thereof, if he dies out of state.

Priority 4 In any county, if more than one, in which the decedent leaves an estate, and he was not a resident or did not die therein. The superior court of that county in which a petition for letters testamentary is first filed has jurisdiction over all of the decedent's estate.

Once the proper jurisdiction is determined, it is then a matter of following accepted procedures therein. Probate clerks can be helpful in this regard (but not always). So, go *in person* to the probate court of jurisdiction, and make preliminary inquiries.

State that you are the will-appointed executor, and that you want to get letters testamentary. Then ask, "How does one go about this?" Immediately add: "I do not want an attorney. I'll prepare and file the papers myself." You probably will not get clear or complete instructions, but you will get some kind of response.

Next, ask the probate clerk where you can procure the required official forms. This inquiry will alert the clerk to the fact that you are aware that official forms may exist. You may be told that they are available at a legal-forms publisher in the vicinity of the probate court. Or, you may be told that you can find the format for such forms in the probate code in the court's law library.

Interestingly, the official forms for letters often show a box at the heading:

Attorney or Party Without Attorney
(Name, address, and phone number)

This wording is an innocuous recognition that a will-appointed executor can prepare his own papers.

You will never find an instruction booklet for preparing the forms, like those which accompany your federal and state income tax forms. The nearest to any instructions are footnotes and other parenthetical notes (including references to applicable sections of the probate code) directly on the official forms themselves. The forms generally consist of short statements (enumerated) followed by check-boxes and blank spaces. In some states, the official probate forms are quite self-explanatory.

Remembering that "probate" means proving the will, you cannot get letters without submitting the will to probate. An overview of the sequential procedures involved is presented in Figure 3.1. Take a few moments and read through Figure 3.1 carefully.

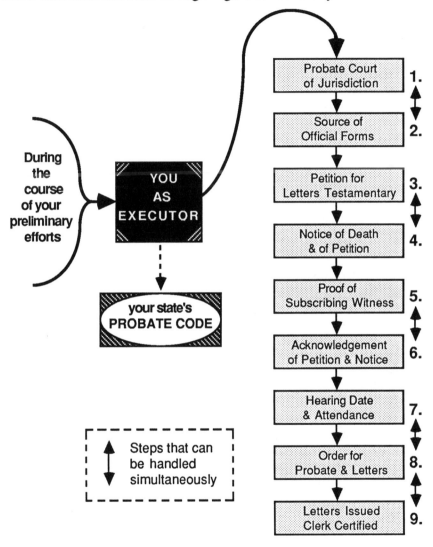

Fig. 3.1 - Sequential Steps for Obtaining Letters Testamentary

First: You Must Petition

We suspect that your first reaction to Figure 3.1 is: "Is all of *that* really necessary?"

Unfortunately, yes. Much of it is purely perfunctory and several of the steps can be taken simultaneously. The letters process is a charade which the legal system is imposing on you — perhaps to intimidate you.

Chances are, the intimidation derives from some specific section in your state's probate code. In California, for example, the law presumes that you have renounced your right to letters if you fail to petition for same. Specifically, Section 8001 (California Probate Code) states:

> *Unless good cause for delay is shown, if a person named in a will as executor fails to petition the court for administration of the estate **within 30 days after** the person has knowledge of the death of the decedent and that person is named as executor, the person may be held to have waived the right to appointment as personal representative.*

The purpose of the above is to permit any distributee of the estate to hire an attorney, and have the attorney petition for letters. This could shut you out, unless you can show *good cause.* Your best good cause is that you have been engaged in the proper preliminary efforts (such as reviewing the probate code) and that it has taken you longer than 30 days to get the necessary information for preparing the petition.

Thus, the first official form that you seek is **Petition for Probate**. This is its "short title." Actually, the more correct title is: Petition for Probate of Will and for Letters Testamentary and for Authority to Administer Estate Independently. Check-boxes on official forms will permit you to indicate this title, without your actually having to write it.

An illustration of what is contained on an official Petition for Probate form is presented in Figure 3.2. It is an abridged and editorialized version of a California form. When you read through Figure 3.2, you'll see why it takes more than 30 days to get the necessary information to complete the form.

What do you do if there is no official form available?

It is a simple matter, though it can be made difficult. You ask the probate clerk for a sample petition that has been prepared by

Name & Address of Petitioner	For Court Use
Name & Address of Superior Court	
Name of Decedent	

PETITION FOR	Case No. _____
☐ Probate of Will　　　☐ _____	Hearing Date _____
☐ Letters Testamentary　☐ _____	
☐ Independant Administration	Dept. ____ Time ____

1. Petitioner requests that:

      a. ☐ Decedent's Will be admitted to probate.
      b. ☐ He be appointed Executor with Letters Testamentary.
      c. ☐ Authority be granted to administer estate independently.
      d. ☐ Bond not be required.

2. Decedent died on _____

      a. ☐ A resident of the county of _____
      b. ☐ A nonresident with estate in county of _____
      c. ☐ Character and estimated value of estate:
            ☐ Real property $ _____
            ☐ Personal property $ _____
      d. ☐ Will waives bond.
      e. ☐ Copy of decedent's Will dated _____ is attached.
      f. ☐ Proposed Executor is named in Will.
      g. ☐ Proposed Executor is resident of _____

3. Decedent is survived by _____

4. Decedent's Will does ☐ does not ☐ preclude independant administration.

5. Names, residences, relationships, and ages of heirs, devisees, and legatees named in Will are attached.

6. Petitioner requests publication in _____

Dated :_____　　　_____ /s/ _____

I declare under penalty of perjury that the foregoing is true and correct and is executed on _____ at _____

_____　　　_____ /s/ _____
(Typed or printed name)　　　(Signature of petitioner)

Fig. 3.2 - Abridged Format of Petition for Letters Testamentary

some attorney before you. All petitions for letters, once filed, are a matter of public record. You pay the photocopying fee and get copy of same.

More than likely, the probate clerk will not be so accommodating. You will be asked to designate specifically which petition (or petitions) you want. In this case, go outside the clerk's office to the public bulletin board. Look for the section on probate notices. Glance through the listings/postings and pick out one or two (or three) that appear to be comparable to your decedent's situation. Record the case numbers. Then go back to the clerk and request photocopies of the case-numbered forms that you want to use as a sample. Pay whatever photocopy fee is asked.

Essential Elements for Filing

Regardless of what form is used, the essential elements in all petitions for letters include the following:

(1) The jurisdictional facts;
(2) Attachment of the decedent's will;
(3) Whether the person named as executor consents to act or renounces his right to letters;
(4) Residence and address of decedent at time of death (including date of death);
(5) The character and estimated value of the property of the estate;
(6) The names, residences, ages, and relationships of the heirs, devisees, and legatees (distributees) of the decedent;
(7) The name and residence of the person for whom letters testamentary are prayed;
(8) Name and location of newspaper where petition will be publicized.

In preparing the petition, the most important formal part is the arrangement of the heading. Whether on an official form or not, be sure that there is ample blank space (at least 2"x2-1/2") in the upper right-hand corner for the filing clerk's stamp. Also, make sure that the name of the superior court of jurisdiction stands out in bold black caps. The name of the petitioner and the name of the decedent should be shown in the left-hand portion of the heading. If you have any qualms on the format and wording on the heading of your petition, be sure to copy *exactly* that which is on the photocopied sample that you have.

Do not be overly concerned about the precision of wording in the body of your petition. As long as the essential jurisdictional facts exist, any defect of form or error in wording can be corrected later. The important matter is to get your petition in, pay the court filing fee, and get going. If some zealous beneficiary or disgruntled attorney is stalking you, this is the first trap where he/she will try to nail you.

When you file your petition (and pay the fee), the clerk will assign a *Case Number*. This becomes your exclusive identification for all legal matters pertaining to your decedent. In addition, the clerk will set a hearing date for the petition. Generally, the hearing is not less than 30 days from the date your petition is stamped: "Endorsed-Filed."

Public Notice of Death

Keep in mind that when you are seeking letters, you are *initiating* the probate process. You may not intend to do this, but probate initiation is essential before the letters can be issued. Once issued, however, you need not necessarily complete probate. Much depends on the character of the estate and on the trust of the distributees.

A key formality of the probate process is publication of Notice of Death. Any person or entity potentially interested in the estate of the decedent must be given an opportunity to be heard. Consequently, the official notification will specify a date, time, and place (in court) for hearing.

Included with the notice of death is Notice of Petition to Administer Estate. Persons potentially interested in the estate must also be informed who the petitioner is, and what role he is to perform. Both notices are combined into one, and printed in the "Legal Notices" section of a local newspaper. The newspaper must be one of general circulation in the city or county where the decedent resided or where his property is located.

Because notice of death and petition is required to be published, official forms for such notice are almost certain to be available. Specific statutory wording has to be used to protect the rights of interested parties. For this reason, there has to be a place on the form for clerk's posting (on his bulletin board) and for proof of mailing (by the petitioner). So, be sure to ask your probate clerk about the official Notice forms.

There is, of course, a legal notices publication fee charged by the applicable newspaper. Publication is required for at least 10 days. The term "10 days" means three publication dates with at least five days intervening between each publication.

For familiarization purposes, an abridged California notice of death form is presented in Figure 3.3. The figure gives you an idea of the formal information required.

Figure 3.3 also is intended to alert you to the fact that you, as executor, are responsible for seeing that a separate copy of the notice is mailed to all heirs and beneficiaries, whether or not named in the will. Even though you may have previously contacted these persons informally, you must now do so, formally. You prepare the mailings, and then have someone else actually deposit the notices in the U.S. Mail. The person who does so has to sign the Proof of Service by Mail . . . under penalty of perjury.

It is highly advisable also to send *each distributee* a copy of the petition itself. You are not really required to do this, as anyone can go to the courthouse and get a copy. However, by sending a copy of the petition, along with the notice, you are making it convenient for the distributees whom you must satisfy later.

Proof of Subscribing Witness

While the notice of death and petition is being printed in the newspaper, you have a related task to do. You have to contact one or more persons who witnessed the signing of the will by the decedent. A valid will must be attested to by at least one witness, preferably two, and occasionally three. Usually, each witness signature is accompanied by the address of that witness at the time of signing.

Your task is to write to each witness at the address shown on the will. Your communication need not be formal: just an ordinary business-type letter. State the fact of death of the testator and attach a photocopy of the complete will. Send your communication by certified mail with return receipt. In the event that a witness is deceased or unlocatable, you want specific evidence of your attempt to make contact.

In your letter to each witness, ask if that is his true signature on the will. Also ask if he indeed observed the signing of the will by the testator, and if he appeared to be of sound mind. Then ask each

Name & Address of Petitioner	For Court Use
Name & Address of Superior Court	
Name of Decedent	
NOTICE OF DEATH AND OF PETITION TO ADMINISTER ESTATE	Case Number : _____

1. To all heirs, beneficiaries, creditors, contingent creditors, and persons who may be otherwise interested in the will or estate of _____

2. A petition has been filed by _____ requesting appointment as personal representative to administer the estate of the decedent.

3. The petition requests authority to administer independently of court supervision.

4. A hearing on the petition will be held on

(date)	(time)	(room)	(place)

5. IF YOU OBJECT . . . , you should . . .

6. IF YOU ARE A CREDITOR . . . , you must . . .

7. YOU MAY EXAMINE the file kept by the court . . .

8. YOU MAY FILE a request for special notice . . . of estate assets . . . and of accounts and reports . . .

CLERK'S CERTIFICATE OF POSTING
_____

PROOF OF SERVICE BY MAIL
_____

HEIRS & BENEFICIARIES TO WHOM NOTICE MAILED

_____   _____

_____   _____

Fig. 3.3 - Abridged Format for Notice of Death and of Petition witness to sign a formal statement, Proof of Subscribing Witness, which you supply. If the witness is in-state, his own signature under penalty of perjury is sufficient. If the witness is out-of-state, he must sign in the presence of a Notary Public.

In most instances, official preprinted forms are available: Proof of Subscribing Witness. If not, ask the probate clerk to show you a recent sample. Photocopy it, then type up a similar form on your own. It is a relatively simple *acknowledgment* form.

Have each witness return his proof statement directly to you. Make it convenient for him to do so by providing a stamped, self-addressed return envelope with your communication. You must have the proof signature of at least one subscribing witness to prove the will.

Acknowledgment by Named Noticees

A "noticee" is the person to whom there was mailed a formal Notice of Death and of Petition. The official notice contains thereon a special clause addressed to heir and beneficiaries. This clause states—

IF YOU OBJECT to the granting of the petition, you should either appear at the hearing and state your objection or file written objection with the court before the hearing.

Any objection by a noticee must be directed to your qualifications as an executor. The notice is not an opportunity to contest the will, nor an opportunity to contest distribution of the estate. The notice is simply a statement of the fact of death, and of your petition for letters testamentary to administer the estate. Rarely are any objections raised at this point.

If you are the sole executor appointed by the decedent in his will, there should be no objection to your being court-confirmed as such. The notice itself is silent on what a noticee is to do if he/she has no objection. Silence or nonappearance at the hearing is legally construed to mean consent. But you want a more positive assertion of consent.

Approximately two weeks before the hearing date set forth in the notice, contact informally each noticee. Ask if he received the official notice. Include in your communication a prepared (typewritten) acknowledgment which you request each noticee to sign and return. Send two typewritten copies: one to be signed and returned to you; the other copy for each noticee's own record.

There are no official acknowledgment forms available. Therefore, prepare your own. Make up a format with a heading similar to that on the Petition and Notice. Then type in a statement such as:

This acknowledges receipt of Notice of Death of __(name of decedent)__ and of Petition to Administer Estate. I have no objection to granting the petition.

____(date)____	*_____(signature)_____*
____(place)____	*____(typed or printed name)____*

If the noticee is in-state, his signature alone is sufficient. If out-of-state, his signature has to be notarized.

If the noticee is a minor, the natural (or appointed) guardian should sign. If the noticee is disabled, the person having power of attorney should sign. If the noticee is incompetent or senile, the appointed conservator should sign. If the noticee is a charitable institution or other incorporated entity, an officer of the entity signs. Be sure that all acknowledgments are returned to you.

No less than three business days before the hearing date, take all the acknowledgments and file them with the probate clerk. At the same time, make inquiry into the status of your case. Particularly ask: "Do all papers appear to be in order at this time? Has the 'Proof of Publication' come in?" (The proof of publication is prepared by the newspaper which ran the Notice of Death; the three actual dates of publication are certified thereon.)

Visiting the clerk's office ahead of time gives you an opportunity to observe if the clerk has done his job in getting matters ready for the hearing. If some papers are missing or incomplete, this gives the clerk opportunity to let you know in time to perfect them.

Your Appearance at the Hearing

Please do not get yourself worked up over appearing in superior court for a "hearing" on your petition. The occasion is more of a non-hearing than an actual hearing. If all papers are in order, including the proof-of-publication and no-objection acknowledgments, the occasion is a *calendar call* only.

The case number is called . . . followed by the name of the decedent. On rare occasions, the court will ask: "Anyone here who objects to granting of letters to petitioner named _____?"

More commonly, there is a short silence after the case and name are called. Thereupon, the judge scribbles his signature on an **Order for Probate.** Immediately afterwards, the court clerk stamps the judge's name on the order and dates it.

The order for probate is a stereotyped form which repeats the date of hearing and says:

THE COURT FINDS that:

1. *All notices required by law have been given.*
2. *Decedent died on _____ , a resident of the county of _____ , state of _____ (or a nonresident of the state, leaving an estate in the county of _____).*
3. *The decedent's will dated _____ was admitted to probate by Minute Order on _____.*

IT IS ORDERED that:

4. *__(Your name)__ be appointed as executor of decedent's will, and letters shall issue upon qualification.*
5. *Authority is granted to administer the estate independently of court supervision.*
6. *Bond is not required.*
7. *The probate referee (inventory appraiser) shall be __(approved appraiser's name)__.*

___(dated)___   _____/s/_____
                                Judge of the Superior Court

Depending on each county's superior court procedures, the Order for Probate is usually a preprinted official form. The form is supposed to be prepared by the probate clerk. However, they expect the executor to do all of the preparatory work. Consequently, well before the hearing, obtain an official form, type in the proper jurisdictional facts, check the right boxes, enter the right names, and affix the right dates. Do everything except entering the judge's signature and date. You can even enter his name, if you know it or can obtain it. Being a temporary clerk's assistant is a learning experience in itself.

Get 3 Copies of "Letters"

Do not be subdued by the impact sound of "Order for Probate." It primarily is a directive to the court clerks to issue you officially, letters testamentary. The judge himself/herself does not issue the letters. The letters are a separate self-contained document of their own.

For letters testamentary, official forms are available. The reason for this is that the letters are a document from the court itself. Specific wording must be used, and statutory requirements must be met. Blank spaces are provided for jurisdictional facts, names, and dates. Here again, you are expected to be the clerk's helper.

An almost exact replica of the official form for California letters is presented in Figure 3.4. A few blank spaces have been condensed and a few words have been edited out, so that the form will fit on the text page. The forms themselves are standard sheet sizes used in ordinary business: namely, 8-1/2" x 11".

Note in Figure 3.4 that there is a section labeled "Affirmation." This is where your signature appears, affirming that you will perform the duties of executor according to law. You may sign and date it in advance of the hearing.

One of your "unwritten" duties is to prepare the letters for the clerk. Fill in everything: the case number, jurisdictional facts, your name, and check the boxes that you want to apply. Have everything ready for the clerk to sign, including reproducible original-looking photocopies for certification. To allow time for correction of any defects, you should present to the clerk your filled-out letters testamentary at least a week before the hearing date.

When you submit the prepared letters to the clerk, you may be asked to indicate the number of certified copies (with official seal) that you want. Without equivocation, order three copies. There will be a certification fee for each copy ordered. The copies will not be given to you until after the hearing.

Depending on local courtroom practices, you yourself may pick up your entire case file from the courtroom clerk at the hearing, and personally take it to the office of the probate clerk. Not only does this save time, it keeps you on top of matters. Seeing this, the probate clerk is more apt to give you prompt attention. He/she will signaturize, date, stamp, and emboss seal the three copies of letters that you ordered, and you can walk away with them.

Why three certified copies?

Petitioner's Name: Address:　　　　　Business hours 　　　　　　　　　phone no. **SUPERIOR COURT OF CALIFORNIA** 　　**COUNTY OF**_____ Address:	For Court Use
Estate of_____ 　　　　　　**Decedent**	Date of Death:
LETTERS TESTAMENTARY	Case Number:

1. ☐ *The Last Will of the above named decedent having been proved, the court appoints* _____ 　　☐ Executor 2. ☐ *The court appoints* _____ 　　☐ Administrator 3. ☐ *The personal representative is authorized to administer the estate under the Independent Administration of Estates Act* 　☐ *WITH full authority* 　☐ *WITHOUT authority to sell or exchange real property.* 　　OFFICIAL SEAL	4.　　　AFFIRMATION *I solemnly affirm that I will perform the duties of personal representative according to law.* Executed on ____(date)____ At ____(place)____ ____/s/____ Personal Representative 5.　　　CERTIFICATION *I certify that this document is a correct copy of the original on file in my office, and that the letters issued the above-appointed person have not been revoked, amended, or set aside, and are still in full force and effect.* Date:_____ _____, Clerk by _____, Deputy 　　OFFICIAL SEAL

Fig. 3.4 - Near-Replica of Official Form: Letters Testamentary

One, you always keep in your possession. It is your "badge" of authority. The other two copies are available for those who insist on original certifications. Otherwise, make multiple photocopies of one of the originally certified copies and use the photocopies freely.

When the Claims Come In

When the legal notice of death appears in the newspaper, one section of the notice reads: IF YOU ARE A CREDITOR . . . (Recall Item "6" in Figure 3.3). This fulfills your duty to notify all creditors. This part of the notice instructs all persons or entities to whom the decedent owes money at time of death to file a claim for payment either with you (as executor) or with the probate clerk.

The actual legal words in the published notice go like this—

If you are a Creditor or a contingent creditor of the deceased, you must file your claim with the court, or present it to the personal representative appointed by the court, within four months from the date of first issuance of letters testamentary. The time for filing claims will not expire prior to four months from the date of the hearing noticed above.

Note that the four months' time runs from the date of hearing on your petition for letters: not four months from the date (or dates) the notice(s) appeared in the newspaper. **No estate can be settled** — no matter what the urgency may be — **until this four month notice-to-creditor time has elapsed.** When adding the prior-to-hearing filing time for the will, witnesses, and petition, it is virtually impossible to settle any estate in less than six months from date of death. The stalkers can stalk all they want. An estate cannot be settled until all creditor claims are in!

As the executor, therefore, your duty is to corral all of these claims that you can. Even go out of your way to make sure that all debts, all expenses, all losses (if any), and all taxes are accounted for and itemized in detail. Unless you question or contest any of the claims, you can pay them as they come in. This is what the estate checking account (in Figure 2.3) is for. Those bills which were regularly submitted to the decedent more than 30 days before death, should get priority.

You are expected to use discretionary caution on all claims and debts submitted within 30 days before death, and at all times after death. You should not pay these too promptly, as you could deplete the estate cash too low. As executor, you *never* want to be in a position where you have to use your own money to pay off the decedent's creditors.

Formal "Creditor's Claim"

If you have any reason to question the validity or amount of a claim, instruct the claimant to prepare a formal "Creditor's Claim (Probate)." There are preprinted legal forms for this purpose. You should get a supply of these forms and send one copy to each questionable claimant. Such a procedure protects you against any personal liability for an expenditure which diminishes the estate.

The Creditor's Claim form has a head portion which identifies the creditor, the name and address of the probate court, the name of the decedent, and the case number. It is helpful if you fill this information out yourself, then let the claimant fill out the rest of the form (front and back).

The front of the form highlights the total amount of the claim, followed by check-boxes which describe the claimant, his legal capacity, and a perjury declaration with his personal signature.

The back of the form usually contains space for a detailed itemization of the facts supporting the claim. If the space allowed is insufficient, attachments are allowed. There is also space for "Proof of Mailing" or "Proof of Personal Delivery" to the personal representative of the estate. Instruct the claimant to return the forms to you: **not** to the probate court. It is up to you to process each claim by getting its approval or rejection by the probate judge (or his clerk).

All claims received after four months after Letters Testamentary are issued to you, are automatically rejected by the court. Be sure to get the court's written approval of the rejection. Thereafter, if the claimant wished to contest the rejection, he has to file a separate lawsuit.

4

INDEPENDENT ADMINISTRATION

As Executor "With Authority," You Can Do Many Things Independently To Expedite Settlement Of The Estate. Upon Proper Application And Approval, You Can Sell Assets, Liquidate Accounts, Dispose Of Personal Items, Make "Direct Transfers," Terminate A Business — All Without An Attorney And Without Court Supervision. You Can Do These Things Without The Approval Of Distributees, Provided You Are Prudent, Humane, And Avoid Mismanagement. For "Sufficient Cause," Your Letters And Authority Can Be Revoked.

Back in Chapter 2, in the section headed "Study Your Executorial Powers," the phrase *independent administration* was used. This phrase also was used in Figure 3.2 at one of the checkboxes below "Petition For." And there is reference to administering the estate "independently" in Figure 3.4.

So important is this phrase that we want to devote an entire chapter to it. Independent administration constitutes the basic premise of this book: that you do not need an attorney except in truly difficult situations. We want you to understand the authority that you have, so that you will not be intimidated from using it.

To describe this authority, we will use the California Probate Code for specific citations. Be aware, of course, that the specific wording in your own state code may differ. Many states use the term *unsupervised* administration rather than "independent." The authority vested in you as executor is much the same. There are some states, however, which do not authorize independent administration. Such states require court supervision all along the way.

Distinctions in "Administration"

The dictionary definition of the word "administration" is—

The act or process of administering; the performance of executive duties; the management, supervision, and dispensing of an estate.

From this, it follows that an "administrator" is a person legally vested with the right of administering an estate. An executor, therefore, is an administrator.

There are four distinctions in the administration of estates. These distinctions are:

*   Supervised administration
*   Unsupervised (independent) administration
*   Small estate (without) administration
*   Ancillary (out of state) administration

Supervised administration requires court approval for all of the major steps in the settlement of an estate. This means that you have to submit preliminary and final inventories; you must use court-approved appraisers and auditors; you must get court confirmation of the sale of realty, securities, and other primary assets; you cannot pay debts or distribute any of the assets without court approval; you have to obtain verification of the payment of debts and taxes; you have to swear to the court — under "penalties of perjury" — as to the accuracy of all transactions before the estate can be closed.

In unsupervised/independent administration, you are not required to submit to court supervision. For your own protection as an executor, you may seek court approval on some particular matter. But once you have your Letters Testamentary (**with full authority** for independent administration), your only responsibility is to the distributees named in the will. You must make a final accounting to them, and file only a short-form closing statement with the court.

With authority for independent administration, you have the legal power to do most anything and everything that you need to, without notice to the court. You have the right to do things without posting a bond, if no bond is directed by the will. Most executors appointed by name in a will are trusted persons known to the distributees. In such case, the testator (will writer) expressly states that no bond shall be required.

If the will is silent on the matter of bond, the court may require that a specific dollar amount be posted, or be placed in a blocked account. This bonding is insurance to the distributees that you will not abscond with their money.

How Authority Obtained

In those states which authorize independent administration, every "take-charge" executor should seek said authority. The first step in doing so is to review the decedent's will. If the will prescribes no prohibition against independent administration, one has the green light to go for it. Application (via a petition) must be made to the probate court having jurisdiction over the decedent's will.

Ideally, if the testator had the foresight, he would expressly direct *by independent administration* in his will. Doing so would virtually guarantee that the court would grant the authority. The only qualification is that the petitioner be trustworthy, competent, and prudent in the management of someone else's property.

The application for independent administration can actually start with the Petition for Letters Testamentary. If you'll glance back at Figure 3.2 for a moment, you'll see that it contains a check-box labeled "Independent Administration." It is not imperative that this box be checked at the time of petition for letters, but it is certainly very convenient to do so. The petition for letters and petition for authority can be handled separately. If so, public notice and formal notification to heirs and beneficiaries has to be undertaken twice. Fortunately, the preprinted official forms contemplate preparing both petitions simultaneously.

In California, the preprinted Petition for Letters shows the following check-boxes in the heading:

☐   *Authorization to Administer Under the Independent Administration of Estates Act.*
   ☐   *with full authority*
   ☐   *with limited authority*

In the body of the petition, the applicant should check-box as follows:

Petitioner requests that—
☐ *authority be granted to administer under the Independent Administration of Estates Act* ☐ *with full authority under the act.*

The check-box for "limited authority" applies to the sale, exchange or granting of an option with respect to real property. The box for limited authority should be checked in those cases where real estate of the decedent is occupied by any heirs or beneficiaries. As a compassionate executor, one does not want to sell a residence out from under a needy heir or beneficiary, without court supervision.

If any heirs, beneficiaries, or other interested persons object to the granting of authority, they have opportunity to be heard in court. If no one appears, or if there is appearance and the objection is without good cause, the authority will be granted.

The granting of authority to administer independently is indicated on the Letters Testamentary. This is done by X-ing two of three check-boxes at Item 3 in Figure 3.4. Verification of this authority is by certification by the probate clerk.

Authority Not Unlimited

The Independent Administration of Estates Act was enacted in California in 1974. It appears in the California Probate Code at Sections 10400 through 10600. Selected excerpts from these numerous sections reveal that "full authority" means that—

Upon obtaining authority to administer the estate under this article, the executor . . . shall not be required to obtain judicial authorization, approval, confirmation, or instructions, . . . with respect to any actions during the course of the administration of the estate. . . . When no hearing is required because the executor or administrator does not seek court supervision of an action or proposed action, no publication . . . shall be required. [The term "publication" means in the legal section of a local newspaper.]

These excerpts give the impression that full authority implies unlimited executorial powers. But you know this cannot be. There are various degrees and conditions to this authority. Court supervision is required for—

A. Special "finalizing" situations
  • such as, allowance of executor commissions and attorney fees, settlement of accounts, final distribution to heirs and legatees, discharge of executor.
B. Self-dealings between executor and the estate
  • such as the sale, exchange, option to buy, or encumbrance of property of the estate for the personal benefit of the executor and/or his/her attorney.
C. When requested by the executor
  • such as when complaints or objections are raised by persons having a legitimate financial interest in the estate.

Otherwise, the executor is given a free hand to do whatever is necessary to carry out the wishes of the decedent. In some cases, however, he is required to give "notice" of his proposed transactions to the heirs and legatees. The Notice (not publication) must be in writing for those actions which diminish the distributable estate or which extend the final distribution beyond two years from date of death.

Examples Requiring Supervision

Authority to administer an estate independently carries with it certain responsibilities. An authorized executor cannot be careless and cavalier. He cannot be insensitive to the legitimate concerns of heirs, beneficiaries, and other interested persons, such as creditors, custodians, and the like. Situations can arise when the better part of wisdom is to seek court supervision, whether required or not.

To illustrate the concern, let us cite three specific examples: A, B, and C. These are ordinary situations where seeking court supervision would indeed be wise.

In example A, there are three adult children of the decedent. They are to share equally (one-third each) in the estate. The estate consists of a $300,000 home where one of the children and his family reside. In addition, there is $60,000 in liquid assets. Thus, each adult child is entitled to $120,000 of the decedent's estate. The child living in the residence wants to stay, but cannot afford to "buy out" the other two children. As executor, what do you do? You have to settle the estate in some manner.

In example B, there are 10 distributees (all adults) of an estate with $1,000,000 ($1 million). No real property is involved. The estate consists of readily marketable stock and securities. Two of the distributees want trusts set up for their own children. Three of the distributees want to pick and choose among the securities, and acquire substitutes of their choice. Five of the distributees want all cash: $100,000 each. As executor, what do you do? Where is your primary responsibility: to the decedent, or to the wishes of the distributees?

In example C, the sole heirs are a surviving spouse and minor child. The will clearly designates that the spouse and child get one-half of the estate each. The estate consists of a $125,000 personal residence and $100,000 in life insurance proceeds. The insurance policy clearly designates the surviving spouse as the primary beneficiary and the minor child as the contingent beneficiary. A minor child cannot inherit property solely in his own name; a financial guardian is required. As executor, what do you do?

All three of the examples above are intended to convey only one point: that "independent administration" does not mean complete autonomy under all circumstances. When necessitated, a petition to the court for guidance is prudent. A general format for doing so is presented in Figure 4.1.

Advisory Notice of Certain Actions

In certain transactions, the affected persons must be informed — advised — in advance of the intentions of the executor (with independent authority). The situations requiring this advisory notice are spelled out in Sections 10510 through 10538 of the California Probate Code. The essence wording is—

Prior to the consummation of any of the actions described . . . without court supervision, the personal representative . . . shall advise the persons affected by the proposed action of his intention to take such action. The notice of proposed action shall [give] a reasonably specific description of the action . . . and shall state the material terms proposed.

The actions requiring such notice are the following:

Name

For Court Use

Address

PETITIONER

SUPERIOR COURT OF _____(state)_____

COUNTY OF _____

ESTATE OF   Case No. _____

PETITION FOR

☐ Approval of Sale of Personal Property

☐ Authority to Sell Securities

☐ Confirmation of Sale of Real Estate

☐ Confirmation of Advice Given

☐ Other _____

Petitioner Requests _____

(brief statement of what petitioner wants court to do)

_____

Petitioner States _____

(brief statement of facts upon which to base court decision)

_____

I declare under penalty of perjury that the foregoing , including any attachments , is true and correct.

Executed on ____(date)____ at _____(city & state)_____

_____   _____

(typed or printed name)   (signature)

Fig. 4.1 - "Blank" Format for Obtaining Court Supervision

1. Personal property items which will depreciate or perish rapidly in value if held to time of settlement.
2. Leasing real property for a term in excess of one year.
3. Completing any contract entered into by the decedent to convey real or personal property.
4. Continuing any unincorporated business or venture of the decedent, for more than six months.
5. The payments and terms of any "family allowance" paid from the estate.
6. Investing funds of the estate in other than federally insured bank and savings accounts, and government securities.
7. Borrowing money or executing a mortgage or deed of trust or giving other security.
8. Entering into any contract which is not to be completed within two years.

There is a common characteristic in the listing above. Most of the actions involve an *ongoing commitment*, rather than a terminus of the estate. Unless there is specific concurrence by the affected persons, the actions give the impression that the executor is seeking to prolong the administration. This is not his function at all. He is not an entrepreneur. His function is to distribute and settle the estate as efficiently and as expeditiously as possible. What the distributees do with their share of the estate, when it is conveyed to them, is their prerogative.

If an executor violates the advisory notice required of him, his authority and letters can be revoked. Revocation of letters means that no executor fee can be claimed. "Any interested person" may file a petition with the court seeking an order revoking the authority of the executor to continue administration of the estate. So, attend to your executor duties and avoid the temptations of entrepreneurial challenges.

Transfer of Nonprobative Assets

All estates contain some assets which can be transferred directly to named transferees . . . without administration. These are called "nonprobative" assets. They bypass the will of the decedent because of contractual arrangements before the decedent's death. The most common of these arrangements is property held in *joint tenancy* (with right of survivorship). Almost all states recognize joint tenancy transfers.

Joint tenancy is the co-ownership of property. That is, there are two or more owners, whose fraction of ownership is unspecified. They may be equal or nonequal co-owners: it makes no difference. If the property (such as real estate, financial accounts, or tangible items) is held in joint tenancy form, the surviving co-owner(s) are entitled to recover that property without administration of any kind.

As executor, it is your duty to effect these transfers without advising other distributees of the estate. Each transfer will require a certified copy of the death certificate. It also will require a declaration (under penalty of perjury) or affidavit (before a notary public) by the co-owner(s) as to his/their right to take possession of the property. The transferred property has to be re-titled in the name of the surviving co-owner(s) only. No new names can be added by the executor.

Another form of "automatic" transfer pertains to *community property* (in those states with community property laws) and *tenancy by the entirety* (in noncommunity property states). These forms of ownership are between husband and wife only. When one spouse deceases, the other spouse becomes the legal transferee. Unless complicated by wording in the will, the transfer requires either a community property petition or a joint tenancy affidavit.

These and other forms of transfers without administration are briefed in Figure 4.2. In every nonprobative asset listed, a certified copy of the decedent's death certificate is required. This is why we designated back in Chapter 2 that a minimum of 10 copies of said certificate would be needed.

Particularly note the last item in Figure 4.2: *small estate* transfers. If the **total value** of the decedent's otherwise probative property does not exceed certain statutory amounts, the property can be transferred to the person (or persons) claiming it. These statutory amounts range from about $5,000 (in many states) to as much as $60,000 (in California). Certain lawful persons (spouse, child, parent, brother, sister, guardian, conservator, trustee) can claim the property without administration of any kind. There is required, however, a formal declaration (for in-state property) or a formal affidavit (for out-of-state property). In California, for example, there is a preprinted form called a "Section 13101 Declaration." This follows Section 13100 which carries the heading—

Estates under $60,000; authorization to act without procuring letters of administration or awaiting probate.

"Nonprobative" means : Outside of Will (by operation of law)		
All Transfers Require Certified Copy of Death Certificate		
ITEM	DESCRIPTION	ACTION REQUIRED
Joint Tenancy (WROS)	Co-ownership "With Right of Survivorship" (WROS); any two or more.	Affidavit : Death of Joint Tenant (Notarized)
Community Property (C/P) Tenancy by Entirety (T/E)	Between husband and wife only; where will silent, is implied.	Petition for C/P or T/E transfer; perjury declaration.
Revocable Living Trust	One or more named bene- ficiaries; irrevocable upon death.	Trustee transferred; ac- knowledged by trans- feree(s).
Life Insurance Proceeds	One or more named bene- ficiaries in binding contract.	Application to insurance company; surrender of policy.
Death Benefit "Plans"	Employer pensions, private annuities, Social Security, Veterans Admin., labor unions, fraternal societies.	Application to plan admin- istrator; verification of claimant rights.
Tax Refunds Federal/ State/ Local	Income tax, gift tax, prop- erty tax, sales tax, or death tax; refunds (if any) due at death.	"Statement of Person Claiming Refund Due a Deceased Taxpayer"; IRS Form 1310
" Small Estates" $5,000 to $60,000	Total probative value; claimant is usually immed- iate next-of-kin; no admin- istration.	In California; "Section 13101 Declaration"; other states similar; called "without administration"

Fig. 4.2 - Transfer Actions on Nonprobative Assets

Set Up "Books of Account"

As to the Figure 4.2 transfers, you are not required to report to other distributees, nor to the court, your actions taken. But you are required to make an accurate accounting of **everything** that you do. After all, you never know when some adversary will come out of the woodwork to have your letters and authority revoked. "Mismanagement of funds" is the allegation most frequently made. It is imperative, therefore, that you set up some sort of record-keeping system (books of account).

There is no stereotyped accounting system that will fit every decedent's estate. For example, suppose the decedent had rental income property. Until the property is either sold or retitled in the name of the distributee(s), you will need a separate accounting trail for the rental income *and* for the rental expenditures. Notice that we use the word "trail" (accounting trail). It is not your function to become a detailed rental property manager. All you want to do is be able to trace the rental income which is deposited into the estate checking account, and trace those expenditures relating to that property. If there is more than one piece of rental property, you will need to distinguish between the deposits/expenditures of each property separately.

The same accounting trail requirements apply to all other assets of the decedent. The difficulty is that all trails lead into and out of *one* checking account as depicted back in Figure 2.3. That is, all trails are commingled. Interest/dividend income sources are commingled with rental income sources, which are commingled with the sales proceeds of readily marketable assets. Obviously, you have to set up some sort of system to sort things out . . . down the road.

To help you get started, we suggest that you codify all deposits in a 10/20 series of numbers, and all expenditures in a 30/40 series of numbers. Limit your code numbers to 9 in each series. Start the deposits with Code 11 and, separately, Code 21. End the deposit series with Code 19 and Code 29. Start the expenditures with Code 31 and, separately, Code 41. End the expenditure series respectively with Code 39 and Code 49. It is always a good idea to keep one or two code numbers "unassigned" for unforeseen accounting trails that could arise later.

Simply for illustration purposes, we present in Figure 4.3 an itemized/codified system of accounts that might apply to an ordinary estate (whatever that is). Particularly note that Figure 4.3 is sectioned into two horizontal parts: prior assets/commitments and death assets/commitments. The term "prior," of course, means prior to death. At time of death, entirely different assets come into being: proceeds from life insurance, certain death benefits from employers,

DEPOSITS		EXPENDITURES	
Prior Assets		**Prior Commitments**	
Code	Item	Code	Item
11	Personal income	31	Personal debts
12	Interest/dividend income	32	Interest/insurance paid
13	Sales of nonrealty	33	Selling expense : nonrealty
14	Trade or business income	34	Trade or business expenses
15	Rental income	35	Rental expenses
16	Refunds, rebates, etc.	36	Collection expenses
17	Loan payments in	37	Loan payments out
18	Sales of real estate	38	R.E. selling expenses
19	Unassigned	39	Unassigned
Death Assets		**Death Commitments**	
Code	Item	Code	Item
21	Insurance proceeds	41	Administration expenses
22	Death benefits	42	Funeral expenses
23	Lump-sum payoffs	43	Professional fees
24	Claims made by estate	44	Claims paid by estate
25	Property appraisals	45	Payment of debts
26	Tax returns (all)	46	Payment of taxes
27	Executor advances	47	Payments to executor
28	Distributee assessments	48	Distributee disbursements
29	Unassigned	49	Unassigned

Fig. 4.3 - Example Codification of Accounts for an Estate

and so on. Also, entirely different death commitments come into being. The 10/20 and 30/40 numbering system helps you to distinguish between before death and after death matters, and between deposits and expenditures.

Code 27/47 makes the point that if you advance or spend money out of your own pocket for the estate, you should be reimbursed. It is quite common for an executor to spend petty cash amounts from his own pocket for such items as certification fees, photocopy charges, postage, parking fees, and other minor items. You are entitled to be reimbursed for all such expenditures that you might make. Your reimbursement would be in the form of a check withdrawal from the estate account. But do use discretion. You don't want to be suspected of "milking the estate."

Certified Copies of Will

In order to get Letters Testamentary, you had to surrender the original will to the probate system. There can be only one original. Invariably, there will be situations in which you will need copies of that will. There will be certain tax returns, heirs who have been "shut out," recalcitrant debtors, out-of-state property held by hesitant custodians, and other bona fide requests by interested persons. Once the original is filed with the probate court, it becomes a public document. Therefore, you cannot refuse requests that are plausible.

To meet legitimate requests, you will need certified copies of the will. For this, we hope you retained the "conformed copy" (with all original signatures) that we discussed back in Chapter 1. If you did, your task of supplying copies is relatively simple. You photocopy as many copies as you need, then *you* do the certifying.

The simplest way is to handwrite or type in the upper right-hand corner of the first page:

> *I certify this to be a true, correct, and complete*
> *copy of the conformed will in my possession.*
>
> _signed/dated_
> *Executor for the Estate*

Another way involves going to a notary public. You can request the notary to inscribe such wording as:

> *I certify that this document is a full, true and*
> *correct copy of the conformed copy which was*
> *presented to me by the person representing*

himself to be the Executor of the estate of decedent named therein.

__signed/dated__
Notary Public/Official Seal

A third way to get a photocopied will certified involves going to the clerk's office of the probate court where you filed the original. Ask the clerk to retrieve the file, and to provide you with the number of certifications that you need. This will cost you a fee, approximately $3 to $5 per page. After paying the fee, the clerk affixes to each copy a preworded certification statement along the lines of:

I certify that this document is a full and correct copy of the original on file in my office, and that the executor appointed therein has not been removed or replaced.

__signed/dated__
Clerk of the Superior Court/Official Seal

There is no fixed number of certified copies required. Much depends on the complexity of the estate, and on the number of "show me" persons and entities to be dealt with. Such persons or entities may need copies for protecting themselves against potential charges of misconduct by distributees named in the will.

Employ Attorney "When Needed"

We do not want to leave you with the impression in this chapter that you will never need an attorney. Situations can arise where the employment of an attorney is not only prudent, but can save you time. An attorney may also save you from major mistakes. Some of these situations are presented in Figure 4.4.

In most estate affairs where the will is clear and forthright, the occasions for an attorney are few and far between. But when they occur, do employ one.

A good example is where property is located out-of-state. Each state's probate laws apply only to property that is physically located within its boundaries. This is particularly true for real property, business assets, vehicles (boats, campers, airplanes, autos, trucks)

ISSUE	COMMENT
TRUSTEE FOR MISSING PERSON(S)	If any beneficiary cannot be located (within 90 days), his/her share of the estate must be assigned to a court-appointed Trustee (NOT the executor).
CONSERVATOR FOR INCOMPETENT SPOUSE	Absence of "legal capacity" of a surviving spouse to adequately manage his/her share of the estate, necessitates a court-appointed conservator (NOT the executor).
GUARDIAN FOR MINOR CHILDREN	A minor child under state law lacks legal capacity; a court-appointed guardian for each child's share of the estate is required... until the age of majority is reached.
CONFIRMATION: SALE OF CONTESTED REALTY	Where multiple beneficiaries become legal owners of realty, their financial interests are often in conflict. Court-supervised sale may be the only alternative.
PRESENTATION OF POST-DIVORCE CLAIMS	If divorce is final, but prior-to-divorce will is not changed, there will be "legal battles"; particularly where a marital residence and minor children are involved.
INTERPRETATION OF CHARITABLE BEQUESTS	Bequests to charitable organizations are not subject to tax. This places undue burden on other beneficiaries, who may assert their own interpretation of ambiguous clauses.
INTERLOCKING FAMILY & GENERATION SKIPPING TRUSTS	Interpretation complexities abound; each beneficiary wants maximum money... without tax. Incidents of ownership and control must be clarified.
QUASHING PROPOSED REVOCATION OF LETTERS	Some disgruntled beneficiary or other observer may serve you with an "Order to Show Cause" (why your letters should not be terminated). Need to answer and prepare "Motion to Quash".

Fig. 4.4 - Particular Issues Where an Attorney Can Be Helpful

and large machinery (farming, logging, manufacturing, construction). Other than financial accounts and intangible items, no out-of-state custodian is going to convey that property to you solely on your own request. It is unimpressive to these custodians whether you have letters or not, or whether you have independent authority or not. They are concerned about their own state laws: not the probate court in a state foreign to them. This leaves you no choice. You have to employ an attorney in the state where the property is located.

There may arise unfamiliar matters for which you may want to employ an attorney on a consulting (hourly fee) basis. Note that we use the term "employ" an attorney. This is exactly what we mean. You employ him (or her) for a specific task only. Do not make the mistake of allowing the attorney to assume direction of the estate administration. If you do, you'll wind up working for the attorney. Then, he (or she) will collect extraordinary fees and commissions.

Except in truly small estates — $60,000 or less — it is legally impossible to distribute and settle any estate within four months of publication of Notice of Death. Nevertheless, there could be distributees who do not comprehend this, and want their share now. They often want to exchange what the decedent intended for them for some property or item the decedent intended for another distributee. To get their way, they may take to taunting and stalking you, and become the proverbial "thorn in your side."

In such an event, definitely get an attorney. Pay him (or her) the *full* statutory commission and fees. This will reduce the distributable estate, but you have little choice when dealing with hard-headed, obstinate distributees.

That "Final" Form 1040

There is one matter for which you should not get an attorney. It is the preparation and filing of a *final* income tax return for the decedent. You know, that **Form 1040** (U.S. Individual Income Tax Return) with which you, yourself, are familiar. As executor, it is your duty to see that a "final" 1040 (for the decedent) is filed on time, irrespective of any death tax matters. You file a final 1040 even if there is no income tax due for the death year.

The "final" 1040 puts the IRS's computer matching system on notice. As you know, every U.S. payer of money has to report to the IRS the name and social security number of every payee. When a payee dies, it is necessary to remove his/her social security number from Big Brother's money tracking system. The only practical way to do this is to file a final Form 1040 for each decedent payee.

There are no official forms for notifying the IRS that a 1040 payee has deceased. However, the 1040 instructions for **Death of Taxpayer** say—

> *If a taxpayer died before filing a return . . ., the taxpayer's spouse or personal representative* [executor] *may have to file and sign a return for the person who died. The person who files the return should write "deceased" after the deceased's name and show the date of death in the name and address space at the top of the return. Also write "DECEASED" across the top of the tax return.*

We think a better way is for the executor to hand-enter at the very top of Form 1040 (in the right-hand white space) the notation—

FINAL RETURN (for single decedent)

or

FINAL JOINT (for married decedent)

Hand-print this notation in bold red letters, to minimize its being missed by computer processors.

If the decedent was single at the time of his/her demise, you enter in the regular signature block on page 2 of Form 1040 the notation (again in bold red letters)—

T/P Deceased ____*(date)*____

(The "T/P" means taxpayer.) Then you sign your own name as follows:

__*(your signature)*__ : Executor for the Estate

If the decedent is survived by a spouse, the surviving spouse enters into the decedent spouse's regular signature block: *Spouse deceased on* ___*(date)*_____ , and then signs her/his own name in her/his own signature block. This tells the computer processors that the surviving spouse will continue to file Forms 1040, and that she/he will be responsible for any unpaid income taxes of the decedent spouse.

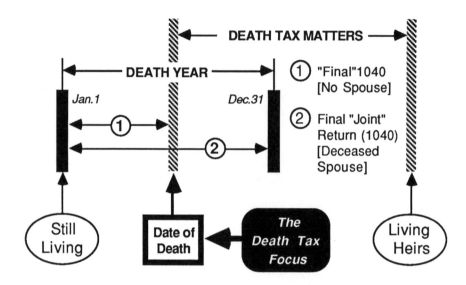

Fig. 4.5 - Year of Death Allocation Accounting Caution

In either case (spouse or no spouse), particular allocation accounting is required for the year of death. This is because the date of death starts a whole new tax ballgame. The date of death becomes the focal point for all death tax matters. Figure 4.5 should help you visualize this focal impact. You want to get the during-life income tax matters out of the way, before you start on the many death tax matters.

5

INVENTORY & APPRAISEMENT

Your Single Most Important Duty Is To Inventory, Appraise, And Determine The Total Gross Estate Of Your Decedent. This Is His Gross Dollar Worth Of Worldwide Assets, Without Deductions. You Establish This Through Comprehensive Inventorying, Fair Market Values, Professional Appraisals, Retail Comparisons, Expert Estimates, Probate Referees, And Actual Sales Within 6 Months Of Death. For Cash Hoards And Life Insurance, Special Tax Forms Must Be Used. Your Skill And Tact Will Be Tested When Probing Into Gifts, Transfers, And Appointments. Items Which Are Non-Marketable Or Doubtfully Marketable May Be Bulk Inventoried.

As an executor, you have many important duties to perform. But, if we were asked to designate your single, most important specific duty, it would be: the inventory and appraisement of your decedent's estate. This is the starting point for satisfying those persons and entities having a "financial interest" in your decedent. In short, determining his gross estate becomes the *baseline reference* with respect to which other matters are gauged.

Taking inventory of someone else's estate is a very comprehensive affair. It means going through *everything* belonging to the decedent and cataloging it. "Everything" means all property and interests of the decedent — his assets, rights, and credits — as they existed on the **date of his death**. Because multiple classes of property are involved, the process can be time consuming. Indeed, your success as an executor will depend largely upon your inventorying and valuation skills. You are permitted to seek professional help from others, as you need it.

The inventorying process should begin as soon as possible after you have established yourself as the executor-in-charge. Upon doing so, all property of the decedent comes under your direct management and control. You must allow no disposition of that property until you have recorded, documented — and appraised — every item in the decedent's estate.

Gross Estate "Tax Defined"

There is one reality of estate administration not well understood by nonprofessional executors. That is, even if no death tax is due, the gross estate has to be determined as if a tax were to be due. The theory is that one does not know whether a death tax is applicable until after all proper grossing procedures have been taken. Thus, as executor, you must be aware that special tax definitions apply which you cannot overlook.

The primary tax sovereign is, of course, The Federal Government. Its position on death taxation is expressed in the Internal Revenue Code. **Section 2031(a)** thereof is especially pertinent here. It is succinct . . . and allsweeping. It says—

The value of the gross estate of the decedent shall be determined by including to the extent provided for in this part, the value at the time of his death of all property, real or personal, tangible or intangible, wherever situated.

Note the phrase "to the extent provided for in this part." The term "this part" covers the gamut of Sections 2031 through 2046. As a handy reference to the titles of these sections, we present Figure 5.1. Also therein, we show the number of subsections (not titles) to each section. Chances are, many of the Figure 5.1 items will not apply in your case. But if any should, you can use Figure 5.1 for making specific inquiries to tax professionals . . . or you can go to the tax code yourself.

Whatever you do, be wary of the phrase: *wherever situated.* This means what it says — anyplace and everyplace, no matter where. It means worldwide. If your decedent has any of the "incidents of ownership" over property (real, personal, tangible, or

INTERNAL REVENUE CODE
Subtitle B - Estate & Gift Taxes
Subchapter A - Estates of Citizens or Residents
Part III - GROSS ESTATE

Section	Title	Sub-Sections
2031	Definition of Gross Estate	a, b, c
2032	Alternate Valuation	a, b, c, d
2032 A	Valuation of Certain [Realty]	a, b, c, d, e, f, g, h, i
2033	Property Decedent Had Interest	——
2034	Dower or Courtesy Interests	——
2035	Adjustments for Gifts Within 3 Years	a, b, c, d
2036	Transfers with Retained Life Estate	a, b, c, d
2037	Transfers Taking Effect at Death	a, b
2038	Revocable Transfers	a, b
2039	Annuities	a, b
2040	Joint Interests	a, b
2041	Powers of Appointment	a, b
2042	Proceeds of Life Insurance	——
2043	Transfers for Insufficient Consideration	a, b
2044	Certain [Marital Deduction] Property	a, b, c
2045	Prior Interests	——
2046	Disclaimers (also Sec. 2518)	a, b, c

Fig. 5.1 - Tax Code Sections Defining Gross Estate

intangible) in foreign countries, in secret accounts, in other persons' names, or in nondomicile states, it *is includible* in his gross estate.

Therefore, no matter where the decedent's property is located, you must find it . . . and place a value on it.

Section 2033 targets those property interests of the decedent which are less than 100%. Quite often, a person may own a very small fractional interest in property, and as such, it tends to become overlooked. Sometimes this is done intentionally, in an effort to conceal property holdings. More often it is done simply as a matter of limiting one's exposure to entrepreneurial risks. Nevertheless, Section 2033 says—

> *The value of the gross estate shall include the value of all property to the extent of the interest therein to the decedent at the time of his death.*

Together, Sections 2031 and 2033 make it quite clear that there is no escape from the all-inclusiveness of one's gross estate.

"Fair Market Value" Defined

Regardless of when a decedent died, the value of every item of property that he owned has some fair market value (FMV). What is FMV and how is it determined?

To shed light on this term, we call forth IRS Regulation 20.2031-1(b): *Valuation of Property in General.* This is an informative but quite lengthy regulation. Consequently, we are going to take only pertinent excerpts from it, namely:

> *The fair market value is the price at which the property would change hands between a willing buyer and a willing seller, neither being under any compulsion to buy or to sell and both having reasonable knowledge of relevant facts. [Said]value . . . is not to be determined by a forced sale price. Nor is [it]. . . to be determined by the sale price of the item in a market other than that in which such item is most commonly sold to the public, taking into account the location of the item wherever appropriate. Thus, [it is]. . . the price at which the item or a comparable item* **would be sold at retail.** *. . . All relevant facts and elements of value as of the applicable valuation date shall be considered in every case . . . for each unit of property. [Emphasis added.]*

The key point in this regulatory definition of FMV is *retail price.* It is not some wholesale or bargain price. For example, suppose the decedent had an automobile. Its FMV for gross estate purposes would be the price for which an auto of the same or approximately same description, make, model, age, and condition could be purchased by a member of the general public. It is *not* the price for which the particular auto would be purchased by a dealer in used cars. Nor is it the price that a family member would pay to take it off your hands.

Regulation 20.2031 is officially titled: **Definition of gross estate; valuation of property**. It consists of nine subregulations, namely:

20.2031-1: Valuation of Property (General)
20.2031-2: Valuation of Stocks and Bonds
20.2031-3: Valuation of Interests in Businesses
20.2031-4: Valuation of Notes
20.2031-5: Valuation of Cash on Hand or on Deposit
20.2031-6: Valuation of Household and Personal Effects
20.2031-7: Valuation of Annuities, Life Estates
20.2031-8: Valuation of Certain Life Insurance
20.2031-9: Valuation of Other Property

We quoted above part of subregulation -1, and we'll touch on others (without quoting them) as we go along. We just want you to be aware that there are applicable IRS regulations for valuating any and all property includible in a decedent's estate.

Role of Probate Referee

As you probably have surmised on your own, there is no fixed, common yardstick for determining fair market value. It is strictly a judgmental matter. It is a judgment based on retail market timing (and/or auction experience), the state of the economy, and the nature and condition of each item of property in question. But whose judgment prevails? Yours, as executor? Some creditor's? Some accountant's? Some broker's? Some attorney's? Whose?

What if there is a contested difference in judgment between two or more persons having a financial interest in your decedent's estate? What happens then?

Here is where the services of a Probate Referee (property appraiser) come in handy. You may employ a referee on your own, or have the court appoint one for you.

Back in Chapter 3, in the section "Your Appearance at the Hearing," we introduced the contents of an Order for Probate. Item 7 thereof stated:

The probate referee (inventory appraiser) shall be <u>*(approved*</u> <u>*appraiser's name)*</u> .

<u>/s/</u>
Judge of the Superior Court

We did not then explain the role of a probate referee. We do so now.

A probate referee is a court-appointed professional qualified to appraise any and all items of a decedent's gross estate. He is a "referee" in the sense that he has no financial interest in the estate. He quotes a value as he sees it, citing authoritative references as necessary. He, therefore, is an impartial judge.

The probate appraiser is also a "referee" in another sense. Being court-appointed, his statement of value is presumed correct. His appraisements, however, can be overriden by contradictory evidence by others who are professionally competent. Thus, if a creditor or distributee — or a tax agent — is unhappy with the probate referee's appraisement, the burden of contrary appraisement rests with the challenger. The burden is *not* on you, the executor.

Probate referees, like all professionals, are entitled to a fee for their services, and to reimbursement for their expenses. Typically, the fee is $1 per $1,000 value of property appraised. This is a 1/10 of 1% fee: very modest as professional fees go. It is (usually) set by state law so that the fee alone will not influence the values assigned.

It is not mandatory that you engage a probate referee for every item in your decedent's inventory. You may designate for a referee's attention only those items which are difficult to establish or where the retail/auction markets are volatile. Such items as trust deed notes, bank/savings accounts, mutual funds, used cars, and the like, you can do yourself. There is no use paying for professional services that you do not need.

Most states prescribe some official form for authentication by the probate referee. In California, this form is titled: **Inventory and Appraisement (Probate)**. It consists essentially of two attachments, two declarations, and a total dollar valuation summary. Attachment 1 with its itemized valuations is prepared by the executor;

	For Court Use
Petitioner_____ SUPERIOR COURT OF_____ Estate of_____ **Decedent**	

| **INVENTORY & APPRAISEMENT** | ☐ Final ☐ Partial | Case No._____ |
| | ☐ Supplemental ☐ Reappraisal | Date of Death |

APPRAISALS

Attachment 1   (Appraisal by Executor) .... $ _____

Attachment 2   (Appraisal by Referee) ....$ _____

TOTAL ESTATE [   ]

Declaration of Executor

Attachments 1 and 2 contain a true statement of ☐ all ☐ a portion of the estate that has come to my knowledge or possession, including all money and just claims. I have truly, honestly, and impartially appraised each item in Attachment 1 to the best of my ability.

Under penalty of perjury -

_____   _____
(typed or printed name)   (signature)

Declaration of Referee

I have truly, honestly, and impartially appraised to the best of my ability, each item set forth in Attachment 2. A true account of my commission and expenses necessarily incurred is $ (commission) and $ (expenses) : $ (Total) .

Under penalty of perjury -

_____   _____
(typed or printed name)   (signature)

See Attachments Hereto

Fig. 5.2 - Edited Version of Gross Estate Appraisal Form

Attachment 2 with its itemized valuations is prepared by the probate referee. An edited version of this form is presented in Figure 5.2.

Particularly note the two declarations in Figure 5.2. Declaration 1 is signed by the executor; Declaration 2 is signed by the probate referee. The total (gross) value of the estate is amply shown. When this appraisal form is filed with the probate clerk, the information thereon becomes public record.

Step 1: Collect & Organize

Now that we have outlined your grossing objectives, it's time to get down to serious business. You've got to start somewhere. So, Step 1 is to go to the decedent's last residence and start searching for, and collecting, all of his personal papers. You need to reconstruct his property life as though he were still present.

The term "personal papers" applies to those books of account, records, files, letters, invoices, payables, passbooks, receivables, check books, title deeds, registrations, insurance policies, business interests, tax returns, and other matters pertaining to the decedent. Searching for and collecting these personal papers is a rummaging process. It involves going through his personal effects, his personal residence, his personal accounts, and his "secret" hiding places, if any. The rummaging should be done very systematically.

You first look for any personal notes or instructions that the decedent may have prepared for you. Some decedents leave quite detailed instructions to their executors. If so, they are likely to be found among his readily accessible files and records. Chances are, they would be labeled "To be opened only at the time of my death" (or similar wording), followed by his name and date of preparation.

If the decedent has been farsighted enough to leave instructions (albeit sealed), you are fortunate indeed. The instructions usually will tell you where to find important papers, and will tell you to contact certain persons and entities. Having such instructions would be great. But don't count on this fortuitousness.

A systematic search (without decedent instructions) begins with locating the decedent's latest income tax returns. Many persons keep their vital records and information in the vicinity of their tax returns. This is particularly so where a decedent has been filing tax returns regularly and dutifully. If you find the latest return, immediately look for prior-year returns in the same vicinity. In fact, your first searching goal is to corral all of the decedent's tax returns that you can find, no matter how far back they may go.

Tax returns tell you a lot about the character of a person. If they are well organized and substantiated with backup records, you have a decedent who has been a methodical person. You should encounter no inventory surprises. He will have most of his vital records centrally located.

More typically, most persons are poor record-keepers. They are disorganized; they set their personal papers down in locations which they themselves cannot find. In this situation, you have no choice but to go through every room, every closet, every desk (or dresser), every shelf, every drawer (including tool boxes, fishing kits, golf bags) and every nook and cranny (including car and refrigerator) that you can find on the premises of the decedent. Look for diaries, bank books, employment records, loan payments, lawsuits, keys, cash, code symbols . . . anything and everything.

After expending your best search effort on the premises of the decedent, go to your own place for conducting executorial business. There, sort through and comb the papers thoroughly. You want to segregate and organize them into specific inventory classes. You need to do this because each class of inventory has separate accounting — and valuation — features of its own.

To assist you in designating separate inventory classes, we present Figure 5.3. Note that we list nine separate classifications. The sole purpose of Figure 5.3 is to help you corral, in an organized manner, all property assets of the decedent. In the right-hand

		Form 706
A.	Real Estate & Trust deeds	Sch.A
B.	Stocks, Bonds, & Mutual Funds	Sch.B
C.	Cash, Checking, & Savings	Sch.C
D.	Contracts, Loans, & Judgments	Sch.C
E.	Businesses, Partnerships, & Trusts	Sch.E
F.	Tangible Personal Property	Sch.F
G.	Life Insurance, Pensions, & Annuities	Sch.D,I
H.	Gifts, Transfers, & Appointments	Sch.G,H
I.	Personal Effects & Memorabilia	Sch.F

Fig. 5.3 - Inventory Classifications for a Decedent's Estate

column of the figure, we show the death tax schedules which apply on Form 706.

Real Estate & Trust Deeds

Many persons have much of their ownership and wealth in real estate. The most common form is a personal residence. Decedents may be owners of residential rentals, commercial buildings, condo units, leased land, farm land, natural resources (timber, oil, gas, gravel), fishing ponds, golf courses, mountain tops, and other, or they may hold "commercial paper" thereon in the form of *deeds of trust*. Whatever the form of real estate holdings, it must be identified in the decedent's inventory.

The most expedient way of ascertaining the realty holdings of a decedent is to pick out the property tax bills from among his personal papers. If a property tax bill is addressed to the decedent, you can be pretty sure that he is the owner or co-owner thereof. It is unlikely that one would pay real estate taxes on property belonging to someone else.

The property tax bill is only a starter. What you particularly need is the *title deed* to each parcel of property owned/co-owned by the decedent. Many executors do not know what a title deed is. They are confused by the mountains of documentation sent to owners by attorneys and title companies. If it is not among the personal papers above, you will have to go, or write, to the County Recorder's Office. The title deeds to real property are recorded in the official records of the county where the property is physically located. Use the recordation number of the title document given on the property tax bill. You must obtain and put in your file the title deed to each parcel of realty owned/co-owned by the decedent.

Similarly, for trust deeds. A trust deed is evidence of money that the decedent advanced to the owner(s) of real estate. The payback of that money is "secured" by a deed of trust (or lien) against the property. There may be first, second, or third deeds of trust, in addition to the primary mortgage. These trust deeds are also recorded in county records. However, since the paybacks on trust deeds are usually made monthly, chances are the documents themselves would be found among the financial papers of the decedent. He probably kept a little payment book showing the balance of principle owing to him, for each trust deed that he held.

Once you have identified every piece of real property or trust deed that your decedent owns, your next step is to determine the

FMV (fair market value) of each parcel of realty. As you probably already know, the value of real estate is influenced by physical factors within the property itself, and by economic factors outside of the property. In addition, the property may be encumbered with contracts of sale, easements, leases, mortgages, liens, condemnations, fractional interests, and retained life estates. So, unless your decedent's property can be sold at its FMV within six months of death, we urge you to pay the fee for professional appraisement thereof. As you'll see later in this chapter, by six months after death you are expected to complete all of the inventory and appraisement.

Stocks, Bonds, & Mutual Funds

Another popular form of property holdings involves stocks, bonds, mutual funds, and similar investment-type accounts. These items are classed generally as "securities," but they include also commodity accounts, option accounts, brokerage accounts, and so on. The idea behind all of these forms of property is to invest an amount of money in the hope that it will appreciate in value; will pay dividends; will pay interest; or will provide other earnings.

The term "stock" encompasses a whole spectrum of ownership interests in an incorporated enterprise. There are various classes of stock such as common, preferred, debentures, and warrants. As executor, your job is to identify all stock forms which the decedent may have, and painstakingly list and describe them.

You also must ascertain the average value of the stock on the date of, or date nearest to, the decedent's death. For publicly traded stock, this is relatively easy to do by contacting a brokerage firm, or by referring to the financial section of a newspaper. For restricted stock (privately traded) or closely-held stock (seldom traded), you would have to contact an over-the-counter or make-market broker.

The term "bond" addresses specific debt obligations of corporations, governments, municipalities, and public utilities. They are identified by a face amount (principal sum) payable on a fixed due date, at a designated (coupon) rate of interest. Here again, as executor, you must pick your way through the bond portfolio of your decedent, and identify each separate bond issue. Each bond or bond grouping has to be market valued.

The term "mutual funds" applies to the pooling of money by many investors into a diversity of stocks, bonds, securities, commodities, and realties. Ownership is by shares (and fractional shares) in a specific fund with a specific objective. Typically, a mutual fund will provide periodic and transactional statements to its shareholders . . . with share values thereon. Most mutual fund managers, upon request, will provide valuation statements for specific dates.

In all cases above, any accrued — but unpaid — interest, dividends, or capital gains to date of death must be ascertained and included in your value listings.

Cash, Checking, & Savings

Sometimes, a decedent will have a "cash hoard" stashed away on his premises, in a safe-deposit box, or in a secured location somewhere. If you encounter this situation, by all means have a witness present. Call to your aid someone who will sign a statement verifying the amount of cash witnessed. The date, hour, and place of discovery also should be noted. Then immediately deposit the cash hoard in the estate checking account which was depicted back in Figure 2.3.

If the amount of cash hoard is over $10,000, the depository institution will ask a lot of questions. This is required by federal law. IRS **Form 4789 (Currency Transaction Report)** is used. The instructions on the back of this form say—

Each financial institution . . . shall file a report of each deposit, withdrawal, exchange of currency or other payment or transfer by, through, or to such financial institution, which involves a transaction in currency of more than $10,000. . . . "Currency" means the coin and currency of the United States or of any other country, which circulate in and are customarily used and accepted as money in the country in which issued.

If Form 4789 is applicable in your decedent's case, be sure to give the decedent's social security number: *not* yours. You are not the owner of the cash hoard.

If the decedent has one or more checking accounts, get a statement from each custodial institution showing the amount on hand as of date of death. Then close each account and transfer the funds into the estate checking account. Obviously, you will need to identify each account with each institution, in your inventory list.

Similarly with savings accounts, time certificates, money market accounts, certificates of deposits, and so on. List in your inventory each financial institution, the account number(s), the certificate number(s), the amount(s) on date of death, and other descriptive data. Get authentic statements/documents from the institutions involved. Then close all accounts and transfer same into the estate checking account.

If you close out any time certificates, there will be some forfeiture of interest. Unfortunately, the forfeitures may subject you to criticism by some of the distributees. So be it. Your foremost job is to inventory and value all of the decedent's accounts as of date of death. This includes any corresponding forfeitures.

Contracts, Loans, & Judgments

Another category of property holdings is what we term "contracts, loans, and judgments." These are arrangements and agreements between the decedent and a private party: either an individual or an entity. These arrangements/agreements are not regular commercial accounts in the institutional sense. They arise from sale of property, from employment services, from trades and exchanges, from personal loans, and from civil lawsuits. Quite often, the documentation on these matters is virtually nonexistent or, at best, is not well coordinated.

A "contract" is an agreement between a contractor (the person to whom money is owed) and a debtor. For example, your decedent could have been involved in land contracts, employment contracts, equipment contracts, servicing contracts, and so on.

There are two sides to every contract. Consequently, there are *receivables* (assets) and *payables* (liabilities). Your decedent could be a recipient of payments, or he could be a maker of payments. You have to distinguish which, and to so indicate in your inventory. This includes the name and address of the other party, the nature of the contract, and the principal amount remaining as of date of death.

A "loan" is an arrangement between a lender and a borrower, whereby money is advanced and repayments are made. Included are personal loans (unsecured), promissory notes (legally enforceable), trust deeds (secured on realty), collateralized instruments (lender holds the collateral), and the like.

Here, again, there are two sides to the arrangement. Your decedent may be the lender, in which case money is due him. He also may be a borrower, in which case there is liability against his estate. You have to identify properly on which side of the lending arrangement you decedent appears.

A "judgment" is a judicial order arising out of a lawsuit between a plaintiff and a defendant. One of the characteristics of life in America is a propensity for lawsuits. Trivial matters and misunderstandings, as well as tragedies and destructions, can produce endless litigation in our over-lawyerly society. Your decedent may not have been immune to civil litigation.

You must determine whether your decedent has been involved in a lawsuit. Do this regardless of which side of the issue he was on. If involved, contact the other party, either directly or through his attorney. Seek to confirm any judgments outstanding and the amount still owed to, or owed by, your decedent. These matters, if applicable, will not go away on their own. They must be identified and valued in the inventory.

In those situations above where money or property is owed to (not by) the decedent, you have an obligation to retrieve that money and property. To fulfill your obligation, you must communicate with each person or entity involved. Do so by *certified mail*. You must insist (demand) that all money owing the decedent be paid to you. You also must insist (demand) that all property belonging to the decedent be turned over to you. Whether you actually retrieve these items or not is not as important as documenting the effort in your decedent's behalf. In any event, the amount of money owed to him, and the value of property in possession of others, is full valued in the decedent's estate.

Businesses, Partnerships, & Trusts

It is not unusual for a decedent to have a direct financial interest in a business, a partnership, and/or a trust. He could be the full owner or part-owner of a small business; he could be a general or a limited partner in a venture; he could be a trustor (grantor), trustee (manager), or beneficiary (recipient) of trust assets. Your duty is to track these matters down, and, where applicable, list them and value them in your inventory.

For example, suppose, on the side, your decedent ran a bicycle and repair shop. If he had one or more employees, you could direct that the business be continued until sold or abandoned. If no employees, you may decide to hire someone temporarily, or you may decide to close the business down.

Whatever you do, you have to go through and inventory all assets and liabilities of that business. In the estate inventory, however, you need only list the nature of the business, the ownership fraction of the decedent, and its "net worth" (assets minus liabilities) on date of death. The net worth should be well backed up with appraisal documentation and estimates of goodwill (which has a value of its own), preferably witnessed. In this respect, engaging a professional accountant may be your best course of action.

If your decedent was in a partnership at time of death, you must contact the managing partner (or successor). A partnership is a business entity of its own. It has its own books of account, depreciation schedules, income and expense ledgers, partners' capital accounts (beginning and ending), receivables, payables, and retained earnings.

As an executor, you should not enter the business aspects of the partnership. Simply request that the managing partner provide you with a certified statement of the decedent's ownership interest and capital worth. The managing partner, in turn, will employ his own accountant to provide the proper information, and will charge the estate for the cost. Your decedent's net interest in the partnership is includible in his gross estate.

If your decedent was involved in a trust in any way, you have some probing inquiries to make. If he was the trustor (the one who set up the trust), did he transfer assets revocably or irrevocably into the trust? If he made revocable transfers, the assets are includible in his gross estate. If he was a trustee, is he entitled to any trustee fee? If so, the accrued amount of fee is includible in his estate.

If your decedent is a beneficiary of the trust, is he a current beneficiary or a successor beneficiary? If a current beneficiary, what are his fractional rights to the trust corpus (principal) and to the trust income (earnings on corpus)? This information and value go into the estate inventory. If the decedent is a survivor beneficiary, has the current beneficiary predeceased your decedent? If so, then your inventory has to reflect the decedent's "survivor's interest" in the trust.

Tangible Personal Property

Tangible property encompasses such items as autos, boats, trailers, campers, airplanes, farm equipment, sports equipment, gun collections, costly jewelry, art paintings, appliances, computers, furniture, furnishings, ornaments, tools, and the like. Practically every decedent owns some form of tangible property. It may be nothing more than a desk, chair, bed, and TV. It is still tangible property, subject to your inventorying canvas and appraisement techniques.

Tangible personal property items are quite easy to inventory. You visit the location involved, and write a short description of each item. Identify the item; state its apparent condition; and, if applicable, give model number(s), license number(s), and registration details (cars, boats, airplanes).

For good organization of your inventory, we suggest that tangible personal property be subclassed into four groupings, namely:

1. Readily marketable
   - vehicles and equipment
2. Intrinsically marketable
   - collectibles and works of art
3. Probably marketable
   - appliances and furniture
4. Doubtfully marketable
   - furnishings and ornaments

We use these groupings because marketability is a characteristic of the worthwhileness of an item to inventory. If an item is not marketable, it should not be inventoried. What you are looking for in an estate inventory are items of value that can be distributed equitably or sold. If an item has no or negligible market value, it can be given away or junked . . . at your discretion.

The readily marketable items should be described in that manner which you would use in a "for sale" ad in a local newspaper. Each item in this subclass should be separately identified. If your decedent had three autos, for example, each should be separately listed. Autos, boats, sports equipment, and similar items can be sold separately. If not sold, you must value each item at comparable prices advertised by dealers and others.

Some items — those in group 2 above — have what is called *intrinsic value*. This applies to jewelry, gemstones, furs, silverware, paintings, etchings, engravings, photographs, antiques, rare books, statuary, oriental rugs, collections (coin, stamp, gun, clock), manuscripts, and other. These items have a special mystique for which no common valuation technique applies. Appraising these items is best left to qualified and reputable experts. Otherwise, federal tax agents will make exaggerated appraisals to cause you endless grief.

The probably marketable items can be "in-kind" (functionally) grouped. That is, large appliances (refrigerators, stoves, washers) can be grouped; small appliances (toasters, blenders, lamps) can be grouped. Furniture can be grouped by the rooms in which it serves (kitchen, living room, bedroom). These items, except for antiques and works of art, are more marketable as a group, rather than as single items. List them and value them in your inventory as such.

The doubtfully marketable items can be grouped as one single inventory entry: furnishings and ornaments. Furnishings would include such things as curtains, drapes, lampshades, wall pictures, and the like. Ornaments would be artificial flower arrangements, book ends, figurines (if not works of art), ordinary vases, ash trays, and the like. You simply must not waste valuable inventorying time on these matters.

Life Insurance, Pensions, & Annuities

Many persons are unaware that life insurance is an inventory item, includible in the estate of a decedent. There are two includible forms. One is on the life of the decedent himself; the other is on the life of a living person, paid for by the decedent. The inclusion items are (a) the face value proceeds on the life of the decedent, and (b) the cash surrender value on the living insured. Life insurance agents rarely make these inclusions clear to their policy holders.

Inventorying of life insurance is not common knowledge. Because so, a special IRS form has been devised to focus attention on it. This is **Form 712: Life Insurance Statement**. To address the two types of insurance includible, the form has two parts, namely:

Part I — Decedent Insured
Part II — Living Insured

A separate Form 712 is required for each separate insurance policy. The form shows all information necessary to identify the net proceeds in Part I and the cash value in Part II.

As executor, your job is **not** to fill out Form 712. Your job is to locate each pertinent policy, and contact an agent of the company which issued the policy. Provide the agent with the decedent's name, his date of death, his social security number, the policy number, and a copy of the death certificate. The agent will see to it that an officer of the company prepares the form and certifies that the information thereon is correct. On your inventory, you simply list the name of the company, the policy number, and the notation: "See Form 712 attached." If more than one form is required, you may want to sequentially number them as 712-1, 712-2, 712-3, etc.

An associated inventory item is the matter of pensions. The term "pension" applies to employer-sponsored and government-sponsored payments to persons in retirement or who are disabled. Ordinarily, a pension stops upon death of the pensioner. However, the pension plan may include death benefits and survivor benefits. Death benefits are a one-time payment after death to a designated beneficiary. Survivor benefits, on the other hand, continue to be paid out — at a reduced amount — until the decedent's survivor dies.

The one-sum amount of death benefits, and the actuarial amount of survivor benefits, are includible (separately) in your inventory listing. But getting the proper information may be difficult. Employer personnel managers and pension plan administrators often are not very specific nor communicative. There is no predetermined form (such as Form 712) that they have to fill out. Consequently, you will have to contact them, and recontact them, to get the estate information you need.

Another associated inventory item has to do with annuities. An "annuity" is a contract to pay out a designated amount of money over a designated period of time. The time period, called *years certain*, may be 10 years, 20 years, — or other. The annuity can start at any age contracted, either before or after retirement. If death occurs before the "years certain" is reached, the remaining contracted amount is one-sum paid to the decedent's estate (or other designated beneficiary).

The amount of an annuity that is includible in the decedent's estate is a complex matter. There are tax-technical formulas that have to be used. These formulas relate to the fraction of the initial contract amount paid by the decedent. Chances are, this information will not be available among the decedent's last papers. Thus, you'll have to do the best you can by communicating with the annuity contractor.

Gifts, Transfers, & Appointments

Probably the most difficult inventory task you will have to perform is to reconstruct all gifts, transfers, and appointments that the decedent made — or may have made — during his life. From the IRS's vantage point of hindsight, it views these matters as "disguises" for minimizing the decedent's death tax. Government, of course, wants to maximize the death tax. Consequently, your attempt to reconstruct these matters by inquiries to beneficiaries and to the surviving spouse (if any), will be met with resistance and impediments. Nevertheless, using all the tact that you can, you must try. There are reasons which follow.

A *gift* is an outright transfer of property for no monetary consideration whatsoever. Once the gift is made, there are no strings attached. The donor cannot get his property back. But all gifts within three years of death are tax suspect. The suspicion is that maybe they were not pure gifts: that the donor retained some "incidents of ownership." Consequently, Section 2035 of the tax code *mandates* that all gifts within three years of death be included in your inventory. You have no choice in the matter.

As executor, you have to try to track down any and all such gifts. This will *not* be easy. You will find very little guidance in the decedent's personal papers. If you are fortunate enough to identify/locate one or more donees (recipients), you probably will not get much cooperation from them. You may even create some animosity. You will be suspected of being a "spy" for the government.

A *transfer* (for inventory purposes) is part gift and part nongift. The proper designation is "transfer for insufficient consideration" (TFIC). The term "consideration" means full and adequate in money or money's worth; that is, fair market value. The term "insufficient" means less than fair market value; that is, a gifted portion. It is the gifted portion that is estate accountable. As a result, all TFIC's made **at any time** during your decedent's life are includible in his estate. TFIC's could be made by the decedent to others, *and/or* by others to the decedent. Ferreting TFIC information for inventory valuation is guaranteed to make enemies for you.

An *appointment* (for inventory purposes) is the granting of power to the decedent to invade the corpus of an account, estate, or trust of another person. Conversely, it is also power granted by the decedent to another person to invade property of the decedent. Here, the term "invade" means the right to consume, use, expend, or appropriate the property (or portion thereof).

To illustrate the inventory concerns over appointments, consider that the decedent had three adult children. He added one child's name to a large savings account; he put the second child's name on the title to a parcel of land; and he made the third child a trustee in an irrevocable trust that he had set up. Knowingly or unknowingly, he has added three co-owners to his property, each of whom has the right to appropriate all or part of that property for his/her own use. Conversely, the decedent may have been appointed by three other property owners to use and consume any portions of their properties. Whether one's "power to invade" the property of another is used or not is irrelevant. The power (right) to do so is the same as property ownership. Consequently, all powers of appointment involving the decedent are includible in the inventory of his estate.

Powers of appointment are highly technical matters. They require thorough investigation and legal analysis. If appointments to appropriate property are applicable to your decedent, you may need professional assistance thereon.

Personal Effects & Memorabilia

Every decedent has some personal effects and memorabilia. These items (except for fur coats, evening dress, expensive suits) have no market value whatsoever. Sentimental value to loved ones and close friends: yes. But as to stranger-on-the-street marketability: no. Consequently, you need not even inventory these items.

Merely collect them and list them as one single entry. Assign some nominal value, such as $100, $500 . . . or whatever. Listing a single entry with a nominal value attests to the fact that you did take into account the decedent's personal effects and memorabilia. Otherwise, the IRS will assert that you are trying to keep valuable items out of the decedent's gross estate.

Personal effects are clothing, costume jewelry, bedding, utensils (except genuine silverware), hand tools, shavers, hygienic items, eye glasses, hearing aids, and the like. Memorabilia include photo albums, diaries, personal letters, artifacts (made by the decedent), trophies and awards, literary efforts, genealogy records, and the like. Who possibly in the retail world would want these items and pay cash money for them?

Nobody.

Therefore, simply gather up all of these items and offer them to the distributees and others, on a first-to-claim basis. In fact, appoint one of the distributees to take charge of these items and dispense with them as he/she sees fit. This is *not* a distribution of property as intended by the will. This is just sound inventory and appraisement practice. You need to minimize clutter and avoid emotional hangups. You also need to know when to stop taking inventory of the decedent's estate. Do you inventory and appraise every pencil and paper clip that you find?

At some point, you have to draw the line. A safe rule is *less than $100*. If a single item or group of identically similar items have a value of less than $100, assign them to a "clutter pile." After notifying the distributees, call in a haul-away service and have the clutter carted to the local dump. Your inventory must show only those items which truly have retail market value. Ten, 20, or 30 items, each of less than $100, is inconsequential in a death tax accountable estate of $600,000 or more.

Alternate Valuation Date

Section 2031 of the tax code (Figure 5.1) requires that valuation of the decedent's gross estate be made "at the time of his death." This is generally construed to mean *on* the date of death.

There are bona fide situations where property, or a portion of it, has to be sold to satisfy creditor claims before all of the valuations can be made. There are other situations where property values change dramatically — up or down — shortly after the decedent's death. Some changes in value are brought on by natural disasters, sudden inflation, economic depressions, bank and business failures, casualties and thefts, and the like.

Section 2032 (Alternate Valuation) recognizes these possibilities. Within limits, an alternate date to the date of death may be selected.

The conditions for selecting an alternate valuation date are set forth in Section 2032(a), namely:

The value of the gross estate may be determined, if the executor so elects, by valuing all of the property included in the gross estate as follows:
(1) In the case of property distributed, sold, exchanged, or otherwise disposed of within 6 months after the decedent's death, such property shall be valued as of the date of distribution, sale, exchange, or other disposition.
(2) In the case of property not distributed, sold, exchanged, or otherwise disposed of, within 6 months after the decedent's death, such property shall be valued as of the date 6 months after the decedent's death. [Emphasis added.]

Particularly note the wording above: "by valuing **all** of the property." The "all" means that you, as executor, must choose between Section 2031 (date of death) *or* Section 2032 (alternate date). You must choose one or the other. You cannot mix the two sections by taking the lowest valuation for each property item. If you do not indicate your preference, Section 2031 prevails.

Be fully aware that Section 2032 applies to valuations only. It does not apply to the inventory. There is no alternative date option for taking inventory. If there were such an option, opportunity for abuse could abound. Property could be secreted from the estate; portions of it could be disguised, omitted, or dissipated. Therefore, the inventory date is statutorily fixed: the date of death.There is also a special implication in Section 2032. Though not stated as such, it contemplates that all valuations be completed on or before six months after death. This is a reasonable length of time for any take-charge executor.

It is not always clear ahead of time which of the two valuation dates — Section 2031 or Section 2032 — is better for grossing purposes. For this reason, some executors will value under both sections: date of death *and* six months thereafter. The choice does not have to be made until after the six months have elapsed.

Putting It All Together

The inventorying and valuation processes cannot go on forever. At some point in time, you have to pull it all together and establish the gross estate. You may select to do this as of date of death or the six months alternate date. If you choose the date of death, only one set of values is needed. If you select the alternate date, you have to show *two* sets of values: one for date of death and one for the alternate date.

Keep in mind that the gross estate is a recapitulation of all *assets* of the decedent. Liabilities are not considered (at this point). The gross estate is the total dollar value worth of the decedent . . . without any deductions whatsoever.

A word of caution when grossing an estate. There may be assets which are physically, legally, or politically inaccessible for full and adequate valuation. For example, the decedent may have some gold coins in a foreign safe-deposit box, or he may have some farm machinery tied up in litigation, or he may have some inherited antique furniture in a communist-controlled country.

Should such assets be in your decedent's estate, you must make your best effort to describe them, and list their valuation as:
- Not yet determined,
- Determinable value doubtful
- Preliminary value only,

. . . or other suitable terminology. The idea is to show that you are doing your best; that you are concealing nothing; and that circumstances exist which are beyond your control.

If the estate consists of nil-value personal effects, artifacts, and memorabilia, do not omit them. As suggested previously, categorize them appropriately and enter some nominal value, such as $100, $300, or whatever. Do not enter "no value" (or "no ascertainable value") even if true. Such entries generate suspicions by heirs and others, and cause them to probe and dig in.

ESTATE OF : (full name)	DECEASED : (date)		
RECAPITULATION OF GROSS ESTATE			
Asset Groupings	Alternate Date	Value Alternate Date	Value Death Date
A. Real Property			
B. Stocks & Bonds			
C. Mortgages, Notes, & Cash			
D. Insurance on Decedent's Life			
E. Jointly Owned Property			
F. Miscellaneous Property			
G. Transfers During Life			
H. Powers of Appointment			
I. Pensions & Annuities			
THE TOTAL GROSS ESTATE ➡		$_____	$_____

Fig. 5.4 - Official Asset Groupings for Total Gross Estate

Psychologically, it is better to enter some dollar value for personal effects — even if a pure guess — than no value at all.

When final grossing the estate, you must use the official groupings on the death tax form (Form 706), if the total value approaches or exceeds $600,000. Otherwise, for disclosure to distributees, you may summarize the estate by those groupings that we presented back in Figure 5.3.

The official recapitulation groupings of a decedent's gross estate are presented in Figure 5.4. As you can see, the very first item shown is real estate. In most cases, this dominates the gross estate. If there is truly no realty involved, do not leave the listing space blank. Instead, enter the value as "None." This puts tax agents and financial interests on notice that there is no real property to attach, should they be contemplating dilatory legal demands.

If there are other categories in Figure 5.4 for which truly there are no applicable assets, also enter the word "None." For some reason, leaving an official recapitulation space blank tends to generate confrontation, long after an estate has been duly inventoried and valued.

6

FEDERAL FORM 706

There Is No Escaping Attention To Death Taxes ... And To IRS Form 706. Certain Estates—Those Less Than $600,000—Are Not Required To File This 35-Page Form. There Are 9 Schedules Of Assets And 6 Schedules Of Deductions Which Should Be Completed For All Estates. There Are Other Schedules And "Probing Questions" Which Require Reference To Official Instructions And To The Tax Code. As Executor, You Should Be Prepared To File The Death Tax Return, Whether Ultimately Required Or Not. The Filing Of An "Information Return" Can Avert Unfounded Suspicions And Allegations.

They assign a *tax-identifying number* to us when we are born; they tax us as children, when we work and save; they tax us throughout our adult productive lives; they tax us when we retire; and they tax us again when we die. The "they," of course, is our Big Brother — the federal government. The final tax we all must pay is our death tax. This is done through Form 706.

Officially, the death tax is called an "estate" tax. It is a tax on the estate left behind by the decedent. One's estate at death is the accumulation of assets throughout life, after all living taxes have been paid. It is another tax on everything that has been previously taxed.

Technically, the estate tax is called a *transfer* tax. It is a tax on the "privilege" of passing property on to one's heirs and beneficiaries. It is not a tax — allegedly — on the decedent himself/herself. This is Big Government's rationale for dodging angry criticism that the death tax is a double tax on one's life-long income and savings.

As executor, therefore, you need to become acquainted with the format and content of Form 706. It is vastly different from any income tax return that you have ever filed.

Introduction to 706

Sounds like a spy novel, doesn't it? Form 706: special agent. Much soul searching and asset probing is involved.

The 706 is officially titled: **United States Estate Tax Return.** The subtitle thereunder reads—

Estate of a citizen or resident of the United States (see separate instructions). [The "separate instructions" say: *File Form 706 for the estates of decedents who were either U.S. citizens or U.S. residents at time of death.*]

A blank Form 706 consists of 35 pages. Yes, 35 pages! Some full pages are detailed instructions which do not require answers or entries. Among these instructions, you are told to attach the necessary supplemental documents. One of these instructions says: **You must attach the death certificate.** Thus, a complete Form 706 consists of 35 pages *plus attachments.*

A very simple estate might have as few as eight pages of attachments. A complex estate, that is one involving extensive assets and interlocking trusts, can have as many as 80 pages of attachments! There is no doubt about it. Form 706 is the most exhaustive tax document you will ever encounter.

Pages 1, 2, and 3 are general, and are formatted into five parts as follows:

Part 1 — Decedent and Executor
Part 2 — Tax Computation
Part 3 — Elections by the Executor
Part 4 — General Information
Part 5 — Recapitulation

Part 1 requires full identity of the decedent. This includes his social security number, date of birth, date of death, place of death, **copy of will** (certified), and whether or not will was probated. If probated: name of court and case number.

Part 1 — on page 1 — also requires your name and address as executor. You are also required to enter *your own* social security number. Why your social security number?

If you collect an executor fee, the IRS's Big Computer will cross-match the 706 with your personal tax return: Form 1040. The cross-match purpose is to assure that your executor fee is dutifully reported on your 1040 . . . to be income taxed.

At the bottom of page 1 of Form 706, there is a signature block which you must sign. No attorney or tax preparer can do this for you. You must sign and date as follows:

Under penalties of perjury, I declare that I have examined this return, including the accompanying schedules and statements, and to the best of my knowledge and belief, it is true, correct, and complete.

There must be no deletions from, or insertions into, this perjury statement. Its purpose is to get your attention and make sure that you read every page and schedule of the form, plus its attachments. Its purpose is also to assure that you fill in the applicable spaces and answer the applicable questions.

Part 2 will be treated in a separate chapter of its own, namely: Chapter 10. We'll discuss Parts 3 through 5 later in this chapter.

When Filing Required

The filing of Form 706 is not required in every case. The requirement for filing depends on the decedent's gross estate at date of death plus certain taxable gifts during life. The official instructions say—

Form 706 must be filed by the executor for the estate of every [decedent] whose gross estate, plus adjusted taxable gifts and specific exemptions, is more than . . . $600,000. You must file Form 706 . . . within 9 months after the . . . decedent's death unless you receive an extension of time for filing.

This filing requirement applies to the total gross estate of every decedent as an individual person. That is, Form 706 is a *per decedent* return. Thus, in the case of a husband and wife dying simultaneously, such as in a car or airplane accident, the marital gross estate threshold would be $1,200,000 (twice the $600,000 figure above). There would be one Form 706 for the husband, and an entirely separate Form 706 for the wife.

For filing requirement purposes, the gross estate values must be determined as of date of death. The 6-month alternate valuation date cannot be used. For example, if a person dies in 1991 and his gross estate at death is $600,001, Form 706 is required. This is so, even though on the alternate date, his estate diminishes to $550,000.

The above filing thresholds apply to U.S. citizens and residents only. If a person is a nonresident who is not a citizen, and he dies in the United States as a traveler or visitor, the filing threshold is $60,000. This is so regardless of the year of death. (The $60,000 figure was the former threshold for all decedents dying in 1981 and prior years.)

The gross estate thresholds above are *reduced* by the amount of certain gifts made after 1976 and before 1982. These were special transitional years when estate and gift tax laws were undergoing substantial change.

For specific reference purposes, the applicable tax law on filings is Section 6018: **Estate tax returns**. Subsection (a) thereof, *Returns by Executor*, reads in part as:

In all cases where the gross estate at death . . . exceeds $600,000, the executor shall make a return with respect to the estate tax imposed.

Subsection (a) has four sub-subsections thereunder, namely:

6018(a)(1) — Citizens or residents
6018(a)(2) — Nonresidents not citizens
6018(a)(3) — Phase-in of filing amount
6018(a)(4) — Adjustment for certain gifts

Subsection (b), *Returns by Beneficiaries*, is rather interesting. It reads in full as—

If the executor is unable to make a complete return as to any part of the gross estate of the decedent, he shall include in his return a description of such part and the name of every person holding a legal or beneficial interest therein. Upon notice from the [Internal Revenue Service] such person shall in like manner make a return as to such part of the gross estate.

In other words, the primary responsibility for filing Form 706 rests with you, the executor. But if you are unable to make a complete return because some person, entity, or government refuses to release property to you, your Form 706 shall include the name (and circumstances) of such person(s). It is then up to the IRS to contact such person or persons and demand a 706 on the property which they hold.

Be Always Prepared (to File)

Sometimes it is not clear that a gross estate will exceed the filing thresholds. This is particularly true where some item of property, such as real estate, work of art, or precious jewelry, has been valued differently by two or more professionals. Also, because all valuations of unsold assets are basically "guesstimates," one is never really sure of the true total if it is just below the filing amounts.

In these situations, the IRS will step in and make its own valuation. Invariably, an IRS appraiser will assign a value much higher than that for which the estate item could ever be sold. Federal agents rely strictly on the position that the valuation burden of proof is always on the taxpayer: never on government. They take this position, even if you engage a state-certified, court-appointed probate referee. In valuation matters, the IRS always asserts that it is above state law.

To guard against IRS overvaluations, it is a good idea to be prepared to file Form 706 at all times. Be so prepared regardless of the total value of the gross estate.

Notice that we said "be prepared to file." We do not intend that you file the return if you are not otherwise required to do so. Always you should be prepared to prove that you do not have to file. The best way to prove your point is to assemble all of the required information into the 706 format, ready to enter it onto the form at a moment's notice. This includes deductions and credits, as well as assets.

Too, there is the possibility that some disgruntled person with a financial interest in the estate may charge that you have deliberately undervalued the assets to avoid filing the 706. He may go so far as to get an attorney to file legal action against you. If this happens, there would be a demand for you to produce a completed Form 706, whether tax is due or not.

In view of the foregoing and other possibilities, we think there are occasions when you should file Form 706 "for information purposes." If the gross estate is above $500,000 but less than $600,000, we urge that you file an *information return*. You mark it as such — in bold red letters — in the upper right-hand corner of the first page. An information return involves no tax; it is simply "for the record." If the gross estate for the year of death is below the threshold filing amounts, an information return is your best proof that it was not required to be filed.

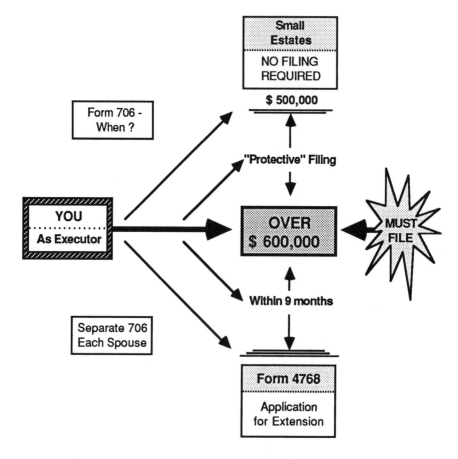

Fig. 6.1 - Key Decisions Relating to Death Tax Form 706

Whether you file an information return or a required return, you must do so within nine months of the decedent's death (Sec. 6075(a)). If you are unable to complete the 706 in nine months' time, you may apply for another six months' extension of time (Sec. 6081(a)). You apply for the extension on a one-page application, namely Form 4768. You must give good and sufficient reason why it is impossible or impracticable to complete the 706 on time.

A pictorialization of the 706 decision-making features facing you (as executor) is presented in Figure 6.1. Note that we characterize an information return as "protective" filing.

General Format & Instructions

It is not our intention that you will be expected to prepare Form 706 entirely on your own. But if you are required to file said form, you are required to sign it (as stressed above). If you are going to sign such a monumental tax document as Form 706 "under penalties of perjury," you should have at least some familiarity with it.

For your introductory familiarization, a highly abridged arrangement of the page contents of Form 706 is presented in Figure 6.2. Note that the form consists of 35 pages. These pages can be divided into four groupings, as follows:

pp 1-3   Front matter & summary
pp 4-20   Asset schedules (for gross estate)
pp 21-27   Deduction schedules (for net estate)
pp 28-35   Credits & other schedules

We suggest that you read through Figure 6.2 rather slowly. It is a good nutshell summary of that which comprises Form 706. In so reading, you may decide that some of the information indicated will not apply to your decedent.

We also suggest that you go to your phone directory and look under U.S. Government Services. Look for the listing "Internal Revenue Service" — and the sublisting: **Federal Tax Forms**. Phone the number given, and ask for a copy of Form 706. While at it, also ask for a copy of *separate instructions* to the form. These separate instructions comprise about 24 pages (depending on the year edition) of 3-columned text.

By simply browsing through Form 706 and its separate instructions, reading the headings and subheadings thereto, you'll appreciate better what is required of you.

Form 706 - United States Estate Tax Return		
Page	**Information Required**	
1.	Part 1 - Decedent & Executor : 10 entries Part 2 - Computation of Tax : 28 lines	
2.	Part 3 - Executor Elections : 5 items Part 4 - Decedent & Beneficiary Information - 5 descriptive entries	
3.	Part 4 - (Continued) 14 "yes" / "no" Questions Part 5 - Recapitulation : Assets & Deductions : 25 lines	
4.	Schedule A	Real Estate
10.	Schedule B	Stocks and Bonds
11.	Schedule C	Mortgages, Notes, and Cash
13.	Schedule D	Insurance on Decedent's Life
15.	Schedule E	Jointly Owned Property
17.	Schedule F	Other Miscellaneous Property
19.	Schedule G	Transfers During Decedent's Life
	Schedule H	Powers of Appointment
20.	Schedule I	Annuities (and Pensions)
21.	Schedule J	Funeral and Administration Expenses
23.	Schedule K	Debts of Decedent ; Mortgages and Liens
24.	Schedule L	Losses of, and Claims Against Estate
25.	Schedule M	Bequests to Surviving Spouse
27.	Schedule N	Qualified ESOP Sales
	Schedule O	Charitable and Public Gifts
28.	Schedule P	Credit for Foreign Death Taxes
	Schedule Q	Credit for Tax on Prior Transfers
29.	Schedule R	Generation-Skipping Tax
34.	Unlettered	Continuation of Any of the Above
35.	Unlettered	Instructions for Continuation Schedule

Fig. 6.2 - General Overview / Contents of Form 706

The 706 instruction pamphlet has many good features. It gives you specific examples of assets and deductions. It tells you who an executor is. It itemizes and explains certain "Elections by the Executor" (Part 3 of the front matter). It gives the death tax tables, and gives numerous examples of entries on the various 706 schedules. On some matters, the instructions become quite technical, such as the generation-skipping transfer (GST) tax.

As to Part 3 of the front matter (elections by executor), the separate instructions go line-by-line on the 706 form, namely:

Line 1 — Alternate valuation
Line 2 — Special use valuation
Line 3 — Installment payments
Line 4 — Reversionary/remainder interests
Line 5 — "ESOP" election

If you are not sure how to exercise a particular election, you can indicate a "protective election" by checking the "Yes" box and attaching an explanation. In most cases, only the Line 1 and Line 3 elections are used. The Line 5 election, for example, applies only to employee stock ownership plans where qualified employer securities assume part of the death tax. Such an election would be rare.

The "Probing Questions"

Part 4 of the front matter to Form 706 is devoted entirely to what is headed as *General Information*. This portion of the 706 asks for a copy of the decedent's death certificate, the certificate number and issuing authority, the decedent's business or occupation, his/her marital status, name of surviving spouse (if any), and the names, addresses, social security numbers, and relationships of all beneficiaries of the decedent's estate. You expect these sorts of inquiries when someone dies.

But there are other questions in the general information portion which penetrate and probe. In fact, there are about 14 such questions. The idea behind the "probing questions" is to cover all estate tax possibilities, no matter how remote they otherwise may seem. Every one of the questions must be answered either "Yes" or "No." Check-boxes are provided alongside of each question. You cannot leave both check-boxes (to each question) blank.

An edited and abridged formulation of the probing questions is presented in Figure 6.3. We want to caution you that the actual

YOUR EXECUTOR DUTIES

	Estate of:_____	General Information	Yes	No
	Please check the "yes" or "no" box for each question			
1.	Does the gross estate contain any Sec. 2044 property?			
2.	Have Federal gift tax returns ever been filed?			
3.	If "yes" to 2: Where filed; What period(s) ?			
4.	Was any insurance on the decedent's life not included?			
5.	Did the decedent own any insurance on the life of another?			
6.	Did decedent own any property as a joint tenant with someone other than spouse?			
7.	Did decedent own any interest in a partnership or unincorporated business?			
8.	Did decedent make any transfers described in Sec. 2035, 2036, 2037, or 2038 ?			
9.	Were any trusts created by decedent during his/her lifetime?			
10.	Did decedent have any power, beneficial interest, or trusteeship in any trust not created by decedent?			
11.	Did decedent ever possess, exercise, or release any general power of appointment?			
12.	Was the marital deduction computed under Public Law 97-34 ?			
13.	Immediately before death, was decedent receiving an annuity ?			
14.	Did decedent have "excess retirement accumulation" in any employer or IRA plan?			

If you answer "yes" to any question, you must attach additional information.

Fig. 6.3 - The "Probing Questions" on Form 706 : General Information

question numbers in Figure 6.3 do not correspond with those on Form 706 itself. However, the sequence of the questions is correct. We have renumbered them so as to better focus your attention.

We are not going to attempt to explain all of the Figure 6.3 questions to you. Some may apply to your decedent; some may not. Some are self-explanatory; some are not. Some are adequately explained in the 706 instructions; some are not. Some are quite complex and difficult.

In glancing through Figure 6.3, you will note that some questions refer directly to the tax code itself. For example, right off, Question 1 refers to Section 2044. What is this?

The instructions to 706 state that—

Section 2044 property is property for which a previous Section 2056(b)(7) election (QTIP election) has been made, or for which a similar gift tax election (Section 2523) has been made. For more details see Publication 448.

Here is a case where the official instructions are not helpful. Either you have to obtain another IRS pamphlet or go to the tax code. In the tax code, Section 2044 carries the heading: *Certain Property for Which Marital Deduction was Previously Allowed.* Now, at least, you know that Section 2044 pertains to marital deduction property.

In order to explain Question 1 fully to you, we have to explain the marital deduction and its estate-accounting involvement. If we were to do so at this point, we would be getting far ahead of ourselves. We will discuss the marital and other deductions in subsequent chapters.

Perhaps, by now, you realize that the overall purpose of Figure 6.3 is merely to introduce you to the depth of expectations on Form 706. Unless you really want to dig into the tax code on your own, you might want to employ a tax professional for some or all of the 706 matters.

"Tax professionals" are those who are designated (licensed) to practice before the Internal Revenue Service. These are attorneys, accountants, and enrolled agents who specialize in tax matters. If you employ such a person, he/she is required to sign page 2 of Form 706 as follows:

I declare that I am the attorney/accountant/enrolled agent for the executor, and prepared this return for the executor. I am not under suspension or disbarment from practice before the Internal Revenue Service. [Emphasis added.]

The Asset Schedules

We previously mentioned that the 35 pages of Form 706 could be divided into four groupings. The second grouping, the asset schedules, consists of Schedules A through I (total of nine). (Refer back to Figure 6.2.) These nine schedules are the *backbone* of Form 706. They provide full disclosure of the decedent's gross estate.

We have fairly well covered the asset features of a decedent in Chapter 5 (Inventory & Appraisement). We see no instructional benefit in restating these matters. However, we do want to point out that there is a Schedule A-1 which we have not previously mentioned. This is called the "Special Use" (or Section 2032A) Valuation Schedule. It applies only to real property, such as farm land, timber land, and buildings on land, where the land is used in the business of farming or other trade or business. The decedent must have owned and used the land in his business for at least five years in the eight years preceding his death. The land must pass to "qualified heirs" who continue the business. There are four pages of subschedules and instructions on Form 706 for Schedule A-1.

The official instructions directly on Form 706 are often quite helpful. For example, consider Schedule F: **Other Miscellaneous Property**. The instructions go on to say—

On Schedule F list all items that must be included in the gross estate that are not reported on any other schedule, including:
1. *Debts due the decedent (other than notes and mortgages)*
2. *Interests in business*
3. *Insurance on the life of another*
4. *Section 2044 property*
5. *Claims, (including refunds of income taxes)*
6. *Rights*
7. *Royalties*
8. *Leaseholds*
9. *Judgments*
10. *Reversionary or remainder interests*
11. *Shares in trust funds*
12. *Household goods and personal effects (including wearing apparel)*

13. *Farm products and growing crops*
14. *Livestock*
15. *Farm machinery*
16. *Automobiles*
17. *Articles with artistic or intrinsic value*

Thus, it is quite obvious that Schedule F is intended to be a catchall. Its importance should not be overlooked because of the word "miscellaneous" in its heading.

The catchall purpose of Schedule F is driven home by several questions immediately below its heading. For example, Question 1 asks—

Did the decedent at the time of death own any articles of artistic or collectible value in excess of $3,000 or any collections whose artistic or collectible value combined at date of death exceeded $10,000? ☐ *Yes,* ☐ *No.*

Do not be misled by the $3,000 and $10,000 valuation figures. They do not mean that you exclude an item or collection if it is less than $3,000/10,000. These values simply mean that if $3,000/10,000 or less, you merely list the item or collection without details. If over $3,000 (for any one article) or over $10,000 (for a collection of similar articles), you must attach an appraisal by an expert, together with details.

Schedules G (Transfers), H (Powers), and I (Annuities) also ask questions. They supplement and reopen the probing of some of the questions in Figure 6.3. Because of the uncommon and unusual information that goes on these schedules, we will expand on their substance in the next chapter.

The Deduction Schedules

In addition to the nine asset schedules, there are six deduction schedules on Form 706. Deductions imply a reduction in tax. This is true. All deductions reduce the amount of gross estate on which the death tax applies. Consequently, everyone having a financial interest in the decedent's estate wants to be sure that all proper deductions are claimed.

The six deduction schedules — J through O — were listed in Figure 6.2. In that listing, Schedule N — the ESOP deduction — is a special case. (The "ESOP" stands for: Employee Stock Option Plan.) This deduction is *temporary* only. In 1986, major tax changes were made in employer retirement plans, forcing the sale of certain securities in those plans. Because new law forced the sale at death, a deduction up to 50 percent of sale proceeds was allowed against the gross estate. The deduction expired in 1989.

As to the other five deduction schedules, we prefer to explain them in some depth in Chapter 8 (Deductions Allowed). In the meantime, we engage in a few commentaries that may intrigue you.

Take the matter of funeral expenses, for example. This obviously is a deductible item. But what are funeral expenses? How extensive can they be, to be allowed as a deduction?

The official instructions provide no guidelines here. So it is up to the executor to document and itemize everything that can be construed reasonably as a funeral expense. This could include travel, meals, and lodging for close family members attending the funeral. All that the official instructions say is to deduct from said expenses any reimbursement paid by insurance companies, employers, Social Security, and others.

The point here is that there are deductions to the deductions. That is, all reimbursement for expenses incurred in estate matters reduces the net amount of deductions allowed.

Another interesting deduction point pertains to income taxes, property taxes, sales taxes, and others. As of date of death, all taxes of any kind (except estate taxes), are computed as due and owing on that date. This computation is in addition to that made for the regular (statutory) due date. If any taxes are unpaid on date of death, they are allowed as a deduction against the gross estate.

If a decedent has overpaid his taxes on date of death, he is due a refund. The amount of refund has to be computed. It is then *added* to his gross estate.

You can be sure that every deduction schedule on Form 706 will be scrutinized by IRS agents. As a matter of foreknowledge, you should be aware that every Form 706 is audited! This is an administrative practice of long standing. Don't worry about it; just be aware. This awareness alone may be justification for your employing a tax professional.

Credit & Other Schedules

Whereas deductions reduce the gross estate, credits reduce the computed tax. That is, a tentative estate tax is computed on the gross estate less deductions. Against this tentative tax, certain credits are applied to arrive at tax due. Credits, therefore, are treated as prepaid taxes.

On Form 706, there are two credit schedules. These are—

Schedule P — Credit for Foreign Death Taxes
Schedule Q — Credit for Tax on Prior Transfers

Both of these credits involve the matter of "double taxation" on the same property items.

If a decedent who is a U.S. citizen or resident has property in a foreign country, that country will levy its death tax before the property is released. At the same time, the foreign-situs property has to be included in the decedent's gross estate. One's worldwide property is includible on Form 706. The net effect is a double tax on the foreign-situs property. There is the U.S. tax *and* the foreign tax.

To soften this double-tax effect, Code Section 2014 allows a partial credit against the U.S. tax for the foreign tax paid. The credit is for

> . . . *any estate, inheritance, legacy, or succession taxes actually paid to any foreign country in respect of any property situated within such foreign country and included in the* [decedent's] *gross estate.*

Schedule P allows you to claim this credit, if applicable, provided you attach full descriptive details.

Schedule Q permits claiming a credit on property which was previously U.S. death taxed. It applies to decedents who have inherited property from prior decedents. For example, a father dies and leaves everything to his only son. Within a few years, the son also dies. Thus, the inherited property is taxed twice: once in the father's estate and again in the son's estate. This situation is addressed in Section 2013 of the tax code.

The amount of the Schedule Q credit depends on the lapse of time between the two deaths. There is a 100% credit if the succession deaths occur within two years of each other. Every two years thereafter, the credit reduces to 80%, 60%, 40%, and 20% respectively. After 10 years, the double tax applies in full.

There are three other credits which are not separately scheduled on Form 706. These credits are:

1. Credit for gift tax paid within three years before death.
2. A statutory exemption credit against the amount of estate tax.
3. Credit for state death taxes paid.

These credits are single-line entries on page 1 of Form 706. We'll discuss these credits in detail in Chapter 10. They have a major impact on the ultimate death tax due.

After all credits are applied, we have to *add* the GST tax, if applicable. ("GST" means: Generation-Skipping Transfers.) The GST tax applies when the decedent has set up special trust arrangements that "skip over" his children **to** his grandchildren. There is a skip-over exclusion (from the gross estate) of as much as $2,000,000 for each grandchild who is a beneficiary of the estate. Such arrangements are attractive for very large estates — upwards of $10,000,000.

The skip-over exclusion is a privilege. Therefore, a special tax applies to this privilege. The rate of the GST tax and its rules are detailed in Sections 2601 through 2663 of the tax code. Schedules R and R-1 are included on Form 706 for showing the computations therewith.

And, finally, there is an unlettered schedule titled: **Continuation Schedule**, on Form 706. The instructions to this schedule say, in part—

> *Use the Continuation Schedule when you need to list more assets or deductions than you have room for on one of the main schedules. Use a separate Continuation Schedule for each main schedule you are continuing. Do not combine assets or deductions from different schedules on one Continuation Schedule. Carry the total from the Continuation Schedule(s) forward to the appropriate line on the main schedule.*

Estates Under $500,000

For gross estates under $500,000 no death tax return is required. If such is the case for your decedent, you need not become familiar with Form 706 at all. But would you feel comfortable without some kind of tax documentation on point? Somewhere along the line, you will be asked to produce a statement in writing as to the total gross value of the estate. What do you do?

```
╔══════════════════════════════════════════════════╗
║        BUSINESS LETTERHEAD OF TAX SPECIALIST       ║
╚══════════════════════════════════════════════════╝
```

TO WHOM IT MAY CONCERN	Estate of _____ *(name)* _____ Deceased _____ *(date)* _____ Soc. Sec. No. _____ Probate No. _____

Verification : No Form 706 Required

This is to verify that on the date hereof, the undersigned interrogated _____ *(name)* _____ , executor, as to the gross estate of the decedent. The purpose for doing so was to ascertain whether the filing of Form 706 (U.S. Estate Tax Return) is required.

Based on documented statements and appraisal estimates presented by the executor, the following assets comprise the gross estate of the decedent.

1. Principal residence : Hayward, Calif. ....$ 221,850
2. Approx. 320 acres farmland : Rush, Kansas............ 86,960
3. Farm tractor & harvester: (5 yrs. old)..................... 24,680
4. Checking acct. : Interstate Bank............................ 17,993
5. Savings acct. : Glendale Federal............................ 49,210
6. Life insurance proceeds : Prudential....................... 50,000
7. Grand piano: (Schiller - 1935) appraised................ 1,800
8. Household furniture & furnishings........................... 1,500
9. Personal clothing & effects.................................... 250

$ 454,243

The instructions for Form 706 require no filing for gross estates of $ 600,000 or less for decedents dying in 1987 and later. Hence, NO FORM 706 IS REQUIRED for the decedent herein.

Date: _____   _____ (signature) _____

 printed name & occupation

Fig. 6.4 - Example Certification of Assets of Small Estates

The answer: You employ a disinterested third-party to provide you with *verification* that no Form 706 is required. You also have said party provide a written summary and listing of all assets of the estate. Before you can settle and legally close an estate, you need a summary statement with respect to Federal death tax thereon.

There is no official form for verifying that "No Form 706 is required." We urge you, therefore, to employ a tax specialist to prepare an appropriate statement on his or her business letterhead. The statement should list all assets of the estate at their "highest most probable" values. We urge the high-side of appraisals for conservative reasons. An example of the kind of verified statement that we have in mind is presented in Figure 6.4. Note that we classify estates under $500,000 as "small estates."

Each tax professional will have his own way of verifying the valuations and describing the assets that he has reviewed. Nevertheless, whatever document is prepared will be by someone other than yourself. Such a document (as in Figure 6.4) can protect you against unwarranted allegations by persons waiting in the wings to trap you.

Particularly note in Figure 6.4 that no deduction items are shown. It is the *gross* estate — not the net distributable estate — that determines whether Form 706 is required.

Correctly speaking, gross estates of $600,000 or less (including adjusted taxable gifts) do not require Form 706. However, for estates over $500,000 which do not exceed $600,000, we urge the filing of an *information* return. An information filing could be particularly prudent for an estate with multiple realty assets, or where there is possibility of during-life taxable gifts having been made without sufficient documentation. Estates between $500,000 and $600,000 could become contentious, should any lapse of judgment unravel.

7

UNFAMILIAR MATTERS

To Complete The Gross Estate Entries On Form 706, You Need To Know About Section 2044 Property, the Q/TIP Election, Beneficial Interests, And Other "Prior Interest" Matters. You Need To Retrace All Transfers For "Insufficient Consideration" Ever Made By The Decedent During His Life. If Your Decedent Has "Power of Appointment" In A Trust, You Have To Include All Trust Assets Into His Estate. A "Qualified Disclaimer" Can Free The Estate Of Property Intended For Your Decedent By Others.

In this chapter, we want to focus on those items in the gross estate that are unfamiliar to nonprofessional executors. Virtually everyone knows something about real property, stocks and bonds, mortgages and notes, cash and savings accounts, life insurance, personal property items, and so on. But what about Section 2044 property, for example? How many persons know what such property is? Very few indeed. It is uncommon estate knowledge.

Focusing on unusual/uncommon items in the gross estate is necessary for three reasons. For one, you will not be able to complete Form 706 without at least an introductory knowledge of the unfamiliar. Secondly, at least one of the items discussed below will — most likely — be applicable to your decedent's estate. Thirdly, you can be sure that federal revenue agents will probe and reprobe all unfamiliar items . . . to maximize the death tax.

In effect, what we are doing in this chapter is going back and reviewing some of the "probing questions" in Figure 6.3 and others on Form 706. We want to provide you with some additional guidance for answering them.

Section 2044 Property Explained

The very first probing question in Figure 6.3 is:

Does the gross estate contain any Section 2044 property?
☐ *Yes,* ☐ *No.*

If you look to the official instructions for clarification, you will find reference to Sections 2056(b)(7) and 2523(a) of the tax code. These references will confuse you more than they will inform you. Your next source for clarification is Section 2044 itself.

Section 2044(a) introduces the concept of "a qualifying income interest for life." Specifically, this section states that—

The value of the gross estate shall include the value of any property . . . in which the decedent had a qualifying income interest for life.

The question that you will ask yourself is: What is "qualifying income interest for life" property?

Answer: It is property in which the decedent's interest terminates upon his death, and passes to some predesignated beneficiary not specified by the decedent. It is property belonging to some predeceased person who permits the decedent to enjoy its income for the decedent's life, after which it passes to the beneficiary (or beneficiaries) designated by the predeceased person. Because the decedent has no power to appoint or designate the ultimate beneficiary, it is called *terminable interest property*, or TIP-property for short.

A typical situation is a husband and wife with adult children. At time of death, each spouse has a separate estate of his or her own. The husband dies first, leaving a life estate interest in his property to his wife. He — not the wife — designates that upon his wife's death the property shall go to the children. The arrangement is made through various contractual forms such as life estate grant deeds, interlocking marital trusts, charitable remainder trusts, private annuities, and other assignments.

Ordinarily, the property in which a life income interest is assigned by a predecedent is not included in the decedent's gross estate. Any asset acquired by the income is included, but not the property corpus or principal itself. This is because the corpus already has been death taxed to the predecedent.

However, in the case of spouses a special situation arises. A predecedent spouse is entitled to an unlimited marital deduction. That is, the predecedent spouse can bequeath to the surviving spouse any or all of his separate estate. If he does so, he gets a statutory deduction which reduces the taxable amount of his estate. An exception applies where any part of the marital deduction consists of TIP-property, which is a life estate to the surviving spouse. TIP-property does not qualify for the marital deduction.

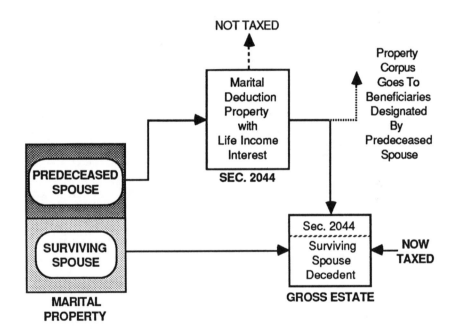

Fig. 7.1 - Pictorial Concept of Section 2044 Property

But there is an exception to the exception. If it is *qualifying* TIP-property (called Q/TIP), it can be deducted from the predeceased spouse's estate. Q/TIP-property qualifies for the marital deduction only if it is included in the surviving spouse's estate. The arrangement is depicted in Figure 7.1.

In summary, then, Section 2044 property is Q/TIP-property of a predeceased spouse. Its chief characteristic is life income interest in property belonging to the decedent's predeceased spouse. For this reason, the official heading of Section 2044 is: **Certain property for which marital deduction was previously allowed.** It is less technically referred to as "certain maritally deducted property." It applies only to a surviving spouse decedent.

The Q/TIP Election

On Schedule M (Bequests, etc. to Surviving Spouse) there is a statement which, at first reading, appears to be a trick question. It is not. The statement reads—

Terminal Interest (QTIP) Marital Deduction. Check here □ if you elect to claim a marital deduction for an otherwise nondeductible interest under Section 2056(b)(7).

Your first clue as to whether or not to check the box has to do with a "marital deduction." Obviously, if your decedent was not married at time of death, you cannot claim a marital deduction regardless of what Section 2056(b)(7) says. Therefore, if your decedent is not survived by a spouse, you are not concerned with Schedule M.

If your decedent is survived by a spouse, then you need to know what Section 2056(b)(7) is all about. It is a special election to claim an otherwise nondeductible amount.

The substance of 2056(b)(7) is a "life estate" in Q/TIP-property to the surviving spouse. More explicitly, this section of the tax code defines Q/TIP as property—

(1) which passes from the decedent,
(2) in which the surviving spouse has a qualifying income interest for life,
(3) in which the surviving spouse is entitled to all the income, payable annually or at more frequent intervals, and
(4) to which no person has a power to appoint any part of the property to any person other than the surviving spouse.

If so elected, Q/TIP-property "shall be treated as passing to the surviving spouse" and is thereby deductible from the gross estate of the decedent spouse.

This election can only be made by the executor: *not* by the surviving spouse. Section 2056(b)(7)(B)(v) is quite specific in this regard, namely:

*An election under this paragraph [Q/TIP] with respect to any property shall be made by the **executor**. . . . Such election, once made, shall be irrevocable.* [Emphasis added.]

Transfers During Decedent's Life

How would *you* answer the following question on Form 706 (Question 8 in Figure 6.3)?

Did the decedent make any transfer described in Section 2035, 2036, 2037 or 2038 (see the instructions for Schedule G)?
☐ *Yes,* ☐ *No.*

Obviously, unless you are a tax professional or a professional executor, you could not know how to answer. Anticipating this, the question itself directs you to the official instructions.

The instructions say that five types of transfers should be reported. These are:

1. Certain gift taxes—Sec. 2035(c)
2. Other transfers within 3 years before death—Sec. 2035(a)
3. Transfers with retained life estate—Sec. 2036
4. Transfers taking effect at death—Sec. 2037
5. Revocable transfers—Sec. 2038

What in the world are all these transfers? What is a "transfer" described in Section 2035, etc., and why is it important in a decedent's estate?

A Section 2035 transfer is the conveyance of property, property right, or property interest to another person for **less than full and adequate consideration.** It is any change in ownership of property other than by a bona fide sale or exchange. If adequate and full consideration is paid, the proceeds would appear in the decedent's gross estate in some other property form.

	TRANSFERS DURING DECEDENT'S LIFE	YES	NO
1.	Were gift tax returns ever filed?		
2.	If so, are copies of returns available?		
3.	Were any gifts made within 3 years of death?		
4.	Are copies of Item 3 returns attached?		
5.	Any life insurance policy transferred within 3 years?		
6.	Any power of appointment relinquished within 3 years?		
7.	Any life estate property transferred within 3 years?		
8.	Any reversionary interest transferred within 3 years?		
9.	Any revocable power or right transferred within 3 years?		
10.	Any transfers retaining right to designate beneficiary?		
11.	Any retained voting rights in a controlled corporation?		
12.	Any prior transfers deferred until decedent's death?		
13.	If so, was retained interest more than 5% of value?		
14.	Any transfer with reserved right to amend or alter?		
15.	Any rights to transferred property created later?		
16.	Any trusts created involving the decedent?		
17.	If so, was decedent creator/trustor of any trust?		
18.	Was decedent grantor/donor of any trust assets?		
19.	Was decedent trustee/successor trustee of any trust?		
20.	Was decedent beneficiary/successor beneficiary of any trust?		

If "yes" to any item, attach copies of pertinent instruments, such as: life estates, title deeds, joint accounts, powers of attorney, transfer agreements, trust instruments, assignment contracts, gift certificates, etc.

Fig. 7.2 - Check-off Pointers for Includibility of "Insufficient Transfers"

Also considered to be adequate and full consideration is an outright gift. If a bona fide gift is made, and the value is over $10,000, a Gift Tax Return has to be filed. The filing of a gift tax return gives the transferee (recipient) full dominion and control over the property gifted. Thereafter, as in a sale or exchange, the transferor has no further "incidents of ownership" in the property.

In short, a Section 2035 transfer is the conveyance of property for *insufficient consideration*. It lies somewhere between a sale and a gift. As a consequence, the transferor retains some incidents of ownership. The property has "strings attached." As such, there are testamentary implications at time of the transferor's death. Hence, the Form 706 question above.

The instructions for answering the question are reasonably self-explanatory. Rather than repeating them here, we present them in graphic form, highly condensed, in check-box fashion. This is done in Figure 7.2. By glancing down the check-boxes, you can mentally tick-off those which are applicable to your decedent.

If only one of the check-boxes in Figure 7.2 is applicable, you are expected to answer "Yes" to the question. Then you have to complete Schedule G (Transfers During Decedent's Life).

Frustration re Gift Tax Returns

One of the most frustrating tasks that you may have to perform is to track down and identify all insufficient transfers and gifts during the decedent's life. This includes locating gift tax returns, if any were filed.

Persons who make transfers or gifts to family members and friends seldom go to the effort of documenting their actions. To some extent this is due to lack of knowledge about tax laws. To a greater extent, perhaps, it is due to the hope that no one will find out about the matter. "It is no one's business but my own" is the attitude of most transferors/donors. This self-rationalization is the very reason why estate tax agents probe — and reprobe — the transfer/gifting issue. To a tax agent, an insufficient transfer is a disguised gift. If a bona fide gift was made, there should be a gift tax return . . . somewhere.

When you look at Schedule G, the very first statement thereon is—

Gift tax paid by the decedent or the estate for all gifts made by the decedent or his or her spouse within 3 years before the decedent's death (Section 2035(c)).

You cannot enter the amount of "gift tax paid" unless you can locate one or more gift tax returns. Thus, at the very least, you have to probe all transfers/gifts within three years of death. This includes any transfers/gifts by the decedent's spouse. Transfers/gifts between the spouses themselves are not tax accountable. Consequently, when one spouse dies, tax authorities also inquire into any transfers/gifts by the surviving spouse within the period three years before the deceased spouse's death.

Because of the uncertainties concerning gifts, there is a real trap question on Form 706. You are asked very specifically:

Have Federal gift tax returns ever been filed? ☐ *Yes,* ☐ *No. If "Yes," please attach copies of the returns, if available.*

Particularly note the word "ever" in the question. The *ever* means at any time during the decedent's life! How can you honestly answer the question "Yes" or "No," if you cannot find any gift tax returns among the decedent's papers? You have to embark on an interrogating crusade among family members, relatives, and friends.

The filing of gift tax returns is the most overlooked obligation of all taxpayers. The rationale for taxing gifts is not well understood. It is contrary to fundamental rights of supposedly free citizens. Nevertheless, filing is required. The tax code is very clear.

Section 6019 (Gift Tax Returns) states very specifically that:

Any individual who in any calendar year makes any transfer by gift other than—
(1) [the first $10,000 of such gifts . . . and transfers for educational expenses or medical expenses], *or*
(2) [transfers of any amount to one's spouse],
shall make a return for such year with respect to the gift tax imposed.

Suppose, after much conscientious effort, you cannot locate any gift tax returns. What do you do?

You answer the official question by inserting the word "Unknown" alongside of the Yes/No boxes.

Joint Ownership Interests

Another matter that is difficult to trace after death is joint interest in property held by the decedent and others. A joint ownership interest is co-ownership with right of survivorship. That is, when one co-owner dies, the surviving co-owner(s) acquires title to the property automatically . . . by operation of law. No formal transfer of that property is required. The decedent's co-ownership interest terminates.

Because joint ownership is a fuzzy-grey area of ownership percentages, the tax code requires that 100% of the jointly held property be included in the decedent's gross estate. The general rule on point is Section 2040(a). In pertinent part it says—

The value of the gross estate shall include the value of all property to the extent of the interest therein held as joint tenants with right of survivorship by the decedent and any other person . . ., except such part thereof as may be shown to have originally belonged to such other person and never to have been received or acquired by the latter from the decedent for less than adequate and full consideration in money or money's worth.

Section 2040(b) *excludes* "one-half of the value" of any jointly held property, where the decedent and his spouse are the only co-owners. Thus, where spouses-only are involved, each is treated as owning separately 50% of the property.

In all other cases, jointly held property is 100% includible in the decedent's gross estate. This is so unless " . . . *such part thereof as may be shown to have originally belonged to such other person.*"

This means that, as executor, you have to contact each of the other co-owners of the decedent's property. You have to insist that they establish with documentation — cancelled checks, bank/savings withdrawals, property exchanges, commercial loans, personal service contracts, and other third-party receipts — their actual ownership percentage. Unfortunately, co-owners tend to be careless about documentation trails. Their primary concern is the mutuality of understanding that each owns the property interchangeably. Consequently, if you cannot establish with certainty the percentage of ownership of each co-owner, you have no choice but to include 100% of its value in the decedent's gross estate.

The decedent's estate could very well wind up paying death taxes on property belonging partly to someone else. This certainly is not morally right. But this is the way death taxes go. The inclusion is a form of punishment for co-owners being cavalier about "fixing" their respective ownership interests.

Those Interpretive "Twists"

The Internal Revenue Service has been administering tax laws since 1913. That's some 75$^+$ years of interpretation experience. This administrative experience has produced a "twisting" of words and phrases in the tax code to require the greatest inclusion of property possible into a decedent's estate.

We want to alert you to some of the more common interpretive twists. As an alert executor, you'll be tuned in ahead of time to likely surprises. You have nine months after death to complete Form 706. The Internal Revenue Service has three years to review the form and contact you for more inclusions. Here are some of the terms the IRS may use against you:

Beneficial interests. This is a broad-broom concept to include the value of any property in which the decedent had a beneficial interest of any kind. If title, possession, or control is held by another person, and your decedent derived, or was entitled to derive, any enjoyment, income, or use of that property, it is includible in his estate. You have to establish the fractional interest of his enjoyment.

Defective dispositions. Sometimes a decedent had all the right intentions to dispose of property in a bona fide manner. He did everything properly, except that he overlooked some technicality in transferring ownership. For example, suppose he made an interest-free loan of $50,000 to his niece who was going to college. He told her that if she graduated, he would cancel the loan. She did graduate but he forgot to cancel the loan. However, he made no effort to collect it. Intentions, no matter how noble, do not count. The bona fide act of disposing of property must be complete and proper in every respect. The $50,000 loan is includible in his estate.

Reversionary interests. Property can be legally conveyed to a new owner for a specified period of 10 years or more. At the end of the period, it reverts back to the original owner. If the 10-year-or-more period has not expired when the transferor dies, it is included fully in his estate. The presumption is that it would have reverted to him anyway, had he survived the reversionary period.

Future interests. A future interest in property arises when it is transferred in such a way that its possession or enjoyment by one of the transferees is deferred until a future time. For example, suppose the decedent's wife's parent set up a trust whereby the wife was to get all income for her life. When she dies, the trust assets would go to your decedent (a future interest). But your decedent dies before his wife. Even so, his future interest can be evaluated relative to his wife's life expectancy. Therefore, it is includible in his estate.

Contingent remainders. A remainder is a future interest in property which depends on the termination of one or more prior interests in that property. A contingent remainder is the future right to enjoyment or possession only if a certain event occurs or a certain condition is fulfilled. An example is a diamond-gold ring handed down from grandmother to mother, to daughter, to granddaughter. The contingency is that the granddaughter is to get the ring upon attaining age 20, but only if the grandmother, mother, and daughter have predeceased her. The grandmother and daughter predecease the mother. The mother, your decedent, dies before the granddaughter attains age 20. The diamond-gold ring is included in the mother's estate.

Dower and curtesy interests. A dower (or dowry) is the statutory right of a wife in noncommunity states to enjoy and possess the real property of a deceased husband. A curtesy is the statutory right of a husband to enjoy and possess the real property of a deceased wife. Homestead rights and antenuptial agreements have similar spousal interests as dower and curtesy rights. Regardless of which spouse dies first, the entire value of the property must be included in the gross estate of the deceased spouse.

Local law determines. The question of whether a decedent has any interest in property and the nature of the interest is basically determined by local state law. But if a state law decision on ownership is reached without federal tax authorities being a party thereto, the decision is not binding on federal tax agents. They may make their own interpretation of state law giving "proper regard" to relevant rulings of the state courts.

The power of interpretive twisting by the IRS — and its likelihood of abuses — stems from Section 2045: **Prior interests**. This is an "in-case-I-forgot" catch-all. It reads in full as—

Except as otherwise specifically provided by law, sections 2034 to 2042, inclusive, shall apply to the transfers, trusts, estates, interests, rights, powers, and relinquishment of powers, as severally enumerated and described therein, whenever made, created, arising, existing, exercised, or relinquished.

A depiction of the referred-to sections within Section 2045 is presented in Figure 7.3. The idea that we intend to convey in this figure is that, at time of death, the tax greed of government looms to the fore.

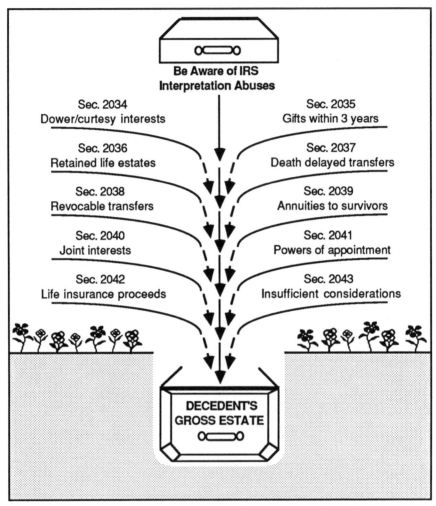

Fig. 7.3 - Resurrection at Death of "Prior Interest" Transfers

Attach Trust Instruments

To most persons, a "trust" is some sort of magic entity that eliminates death taxes, income taxes, probate costs, and estate accounting. Promoters of trusts are attorneys, estate planners, insurance agents, tax professionals, and financial brokers. Trusts tend to be much oversold. They are a death tax trap!

Trusts are the one asset item for which there is no specific schedule on Form 706. There is simply no Schedule T, for example. (The "T" could be for Trusts in Existence) as there is for other assets in the decedent's estate. On all of Form 706 there is just one question and one instruction pertaining to trusts.

The one trust question has two parts, namely:

Were there in existence at the time of the decedent's death:

(a)   *Any trusts created by the decedent during his or her lifetime?* ☐ *Yes,* ☐ *No.*

(b)   *Any trusts not created by the decedent under which the decedent possessed any power, beneficial interest, or trusteeship?* ☐ *Yes,* ☐ *No.*

If you answer "Yes" to either (a) or (b), the one instruction says—

You must attach a copy of the trust instrument for each trust regardless of the size of the gross estate. Complete Schedule G if you answered "Yes" to (a), and Schedule F if you answered "Yes" to (b).

(Schedule G is "Transfers During Decedent's Life" and Schedule F is "Other Miscellaneous Property.")

By attaching each trust instrument to Form 706, you can be sure that federal tax agents will screen — and rescreen — each one. This is because there is much obfuscation surrounding trusts. They are a natural hiding place for assets controlled by the decedent.

Basically, tax agents look for three features in a trust, before deciding what assets are includible or not includible in the decedent's gross estate. These features are:

One.   Assets/interests in the trust retained or construed to be retained by the decedent for life (Sec. 2036).

Two.   Assets/interests in the trust where all dominion and control by the decedent are not fully released until his death (Sec. 2037).

Three. Any power, right, urging, or suggestion by the decedent to revoke, change, or redistribute any assets/interests of the trust (Sec. 2038).

So your duty as executor is to find out if there is in existence any trust involving your decedent in any way. There could be a life insurance trust, an employer trust, an alimony trust, a charitable remainder trust, a marital trust, a family trust, a living trust, a reversionary trust, a grantor trust, a donor trust, a residual trust, or any other. The existence or nonexistence of a trust is not always readily ascertainable. Trusts are private affairs; they are seldom publicized. If you are not comfortable with the evasiveness and runarounds that you may encounter, answer "Unknown" to the trust question.

General Power of Appointment

A rather tricky question in the General Information portion of Form 706 is—

Did the decedent ever possess, exercise or release any general power of appointment? ☐ *Yes,* ☐ *No.*

If you answer "Yes," the instructions tell you to complete Schedule H: Powers of Appointment. Schedule H itself is essentially a blank half-page. The instructions tell you to enter thereon—

The value of property for which the decedent possessed a general power of appointment.

If you answer "No" to the question, are you sure you know what a general power of appointment is? Chances are, the term is unfamiliar to you.

The most common example of a power of appointment is a "power of attorney." In a duly executed instrument, anyone can appoint some other person as his attorney-in-fact. Such appointee can do all acts or do certain acts as effectively as if the owner were personally present and acting. If the appointee can do all acts, it is a general power. If the appointee can do only certain acts, it is a limited power. A general power has all the attributes of ownership except legal title.

A general power of appointment is like a substitute owner. The appointee can do all of those discretionary things that the owner of property can do. The appointee can arrange, encumber, exchange, direct, settle, or distribute property for which he has been granted power. Ordinarily, the appointee does this for benefit of the owner, rather than for his own benefit. When the appointee dies, however, there are implications concerning the exercise of his power.

The fact that an appointee-decedent had the general power "to do all acts" implies that he could have exercised that power in favor of himself. He could have personally consumed some of the appointed property. He could have used the power in favor of the estate. Whether he did so or not is irrelevant. The fact that he held the power to do so is sufficient to cause the appointed property to be includible in his gross estate.

Attach Proper Disclaimer(s)

As the decedent's personal representative, you have one option for clearing the gross estate of any loose cannons in the woodwork. We are addressing prior interests, general powers, and intended transfers of property which you do not know about and cannot unearth. Such matters are rarely found among the decedent's papers. Be introduced now to the subject of (qualified) disclaimers.

As executor, you have the right, power, and privilege of disclaiming any interest in property intended for your decedent by others. You cannot disclaim the decedent's own property or any interest in joint property with others. However, you can disclaim property intended for your decedent by bequest (in someone else's will), by legacy (under local law), by gift, by appointment, or by other transfer. Unless disclaimed, such intended property is includible in the decedent's gross estate . . . for death tax purposes.

To exemplify the benefit of disclaimers, suppose that an uncle predeceases your decedent; the uncle's estate is not yet settled. The uncle bequeathed to your decedent certain property interests; he also appointed your decedent as trustee of a business trust. Without actually knowing what the intended property is or its value, you can disclaim your decedent's interest in that property. If you do so, the property interest will automatically bypass your decedent's estate.

The disclaimer rules are set forth under Section 2518 of the tax code. The general rule thereunder is—

For purposes of this subtitle [Estate and Gift Taxes], *if a person makes a qualified disclaimer with respect to any interest in property, this subtitle shall apply with respect to such interest as if the interest had never been transferred to such person.*

Note the term "qualified disclaimer." To escape inclusion in the decedent's estate, your disclaimer must meet *all* of the following conditions:

1. It must be an irrevocable and unqualified refusal to accept an interest in property.
2. The refusal must be in writing.
3. The written refusal must be received by the transferor of the interest, his legal representative, or the holder of legal title to the property to which the interest relates, not later than nine months after the date on which the transfer creating the interest is made.
4. The disclaiming person has not accepted the interest or any of its benefits.
5. As a result of the disclaiming person's refusal, and without any direction from that person, the interest passes to some person other than the disclaiming person, or to charity.

There is one important caution when disclaiming a property interest, known or unknown. You must be absolutely certain that the decedent himself before death, and his estate after death, derived/derives no benefit or consideration whatsoever from the disclaimed property.

We also call to your attention the fact that there is no provision on Form 706 for disclaimers. Therefore, in order to be sure that your disclaimer is not missed, we urge that you make an insertion thereon. Do this on page 2 of Form 706 in the portion headed: **Elections by the Executor**. There is adequate white space to insert the phrase: *See qualified disclaimer(s) attached.* To add conviction to your disclaimer, have it notarized.

8

DEDUCTIONS ALLOWED

> **Four Schedules Of Deductions Apply To All Decedents. A Fifth Schedule Applies To Married Decedents Only. The "All-Decedent" Schedules Are: Administration Expenses (J), Debts Of the Decedent (K), Losses During Administration (L), And Charitable Bequests (O). The Term "Administration" Is The Span Of Time From Date Of Death To Settlement Of The Estate. Property In The Estate Is Classed As "Subject To Claims" (That Which Is Directly Owned) And "Not Subject To Claims" (That Which Is Beneficially Owned). Administering "Not Subject" Property And Charitable Bequests Presents Executorial Challenges.**

You have probably sensed something from the preceding chapter. Tax authorities endeavor to have you include every asset conceivable, every property right, and ever interpretive twist of property rights, into the decedent's gross estate. That way, Big Government gets a bigger bite out of the estate before distributions to the heirs. It goes without saying: the larger the death tax bite, the less there is for heirs and beneficiaries.

The only legitimate way to reduce the amount of death taxes is to claim all deductions that are allowable. Note that we say "allowable." All deductions conceivable are not allowed: only those which are directly related to the settlement process.

As executor, you have an obligation to seek the lowest amount of tax that is legal. You can do this best by becoming familiar with what deductions are allowed, and which are not allowed. You can be sure that the decedent's heirs and beneficiaries will insist that you do.

"Property Subject to Claims"

In Chapter 6 (Federal Form 706), we introduced to you the deduction schedules: J through O. The first deduction schedule in Figure 6.2 was "Funeral & Administration Expenses" (J). At that time, we edited and abbreviated the official heading. Now we want to present it to you in full.

Schedule J reads officially as—

Funeral Expenses and Expenses Incurred in Administering Property Subject to Claims.

A headnote thereunder says—

Do not list on this schedule expenses of administering property not subject to claims.

This heading and subheading immediately raise the question: What is meant by "property subject to claims"?

From a tax accounting point of view, there are two categories of property in an estate. One is familiar, the other is unfamiliar. The familiar category is property subject to claims. This is that property which is under the direct/full ownership and control by the decedent at time of his death. Any bona fide debts and expenses of, or claims against, the decedent or his estate, are deductible against his directly owned property. They are allowable deductions regardless of when paid. Property subject to claims is the decedent's collateral for his obligations.

The unfamiliar category is that property over which the decedent does not have full ownership and control. He was the *beneficial* owner rather than the direct owner. That is, he enjoyed the benefits of property legally belonging to someone else or to some entity. This property is *not* subject to claims.

An attempt to portray the distinction between property subject to claims and property not subject, is presented in Figure 8.1. Another way of explaining the difference is that property subject can be probated, whereas property not subject cannot be probated. Property not subject is deliberately set up to bypass the probative process. It does *not*, however, bypass the tax accounting process.

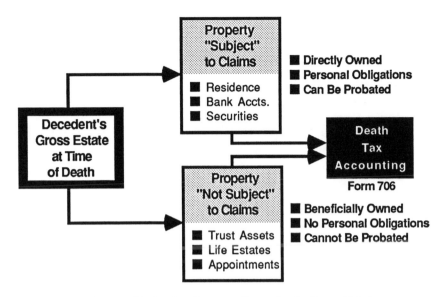

Fig. 8.1 - Distinction Between Properties in Gross Estate

Examples of property not subject to claims are various trusts, life estates, and appointed property. These and other forms of property, though includible in the decedent's gross estate for death tax purposes, are legally owned by some entity, some person, or some beneficiary who is not the decedent. State and local laws generally protect this property against the debts of, and claims against, the decedent.

Section 2053(c)(2) of the tax code defines "property subject to claims" as—

Property includible in the gross estate of the decedent which, or the avails of which, would under the applicable law, bear the burden of the payment of such deductions in the final adjustment and settlement of the estate.

In other words, the governing principle of expense-type deductions is their allowability under local law as claims against the decedent's ownership estate: *not* against his beneficial estate. Many state laws disallow such claims as marital rights, promises of gifts, breach-of-contract allegations, widow and child support, expenses incurred by beneficiaries, and so on. Unless the claim is a personal legal obligation of the decedent at time of his death, the claimants must seek amends elsewhere. Your decedent's estate is not a target for endless foraging by after-death claimants.

Actual Funeral Expenses

Under most circumstances, funeral expenses are deductible in full without hassle. Your principal concern is to carefully itemize these expenses and pay them on time.

In certain community property states, however, only one-half of these expenses is deductible. In Arizona and Washington, for example, state law holds that the funeral expenses of a deceased spouse are a community obligation, payable one-half by each spouse. Most states are more realistic; they treat funeral expenses as the separate obligation of the decedent's estate, whether married or unmarried at time of death. After all, if there is a surviving spouse, said spouse does not incur any funeral expenses on her/his own.

In general, all expenses ordinarily considered funeral matters are deductible without limit as to the amount. Certainly all expenses associated with the determination of death, preparation of the body, and transport to final resting place are clear-cut. So, too, are those expenses for conducting memorial and burial services. These services include the cost of flowers, food, recitals, obituaries, and other directly related expenses. After-burial expenses, such as the cost of a tombstone, its engraving, and perpetual care of the burial plot, also are allowed.

There are some constraints as to what constitutes funeral expenses. The cost of travel, meals, and lodging is limited to one person only. This is the principal person in charge of the decedent's body. For this one person-in-charge, all travel expenses (including food and lodging away from home) are deductible. This includes travel to and with the body; travel to the mortuary and grave site; and travel for tombstone and other memorial arrangements.

There are just three conditions on the deductibility of funeral expenses. One is, there must be actual expenditures: no estimates or futures allowed. Secondly, they must be incurred — and billed — within nine months of death. They can be paid later. And, thirdly, the total amount of expenditures must be reduced by any "funeral benefits" paid by government agencies, employers, insurance companies, or wrongful death proceeds.

As an independent administrator, you are cautioned not to offset the funeral expenses with death benefits, directly. You do this

indirectly through separate accounting categories. This is why —
back in Figure 4.3 — we set up two separate accounts: "Code 22"
for death benefits and "Code 42" for funeral expenses.

Attorney and Executor Fees

Money obligated to an attorney in connection with an estate falls
into three categories, namely:

(a) Statutory commissions,
(b) Extraordinary fees, and
(c) Contingent fees.

Statutory commissions are those set forth in the probate code of
the state of jurisdiction. They are a fixed percentage of total value of
the gross estate. Typically, they average around 2% (3% for estates
less than $100,000 to 1% for estates over $3,000,000). Though
some attorneys will agree to reduce their commission, the schedule
itself is set by state law (which attorneys draw up) and there is very
little negotiation you can do concerning the dollar amount. The
commission covers only that routine/ordinary effort necessary to
settle an estate.

Extraordinary fees are associated with contested matters and
disputes, and unforeseen difficulties in estate affairs. Out-of-
ordinary problems can arise concerning special-use valuations,
questionable obligations of the decedent, interpretation of fuzzy-
worded clauses in the decedent's will, and challenges by heirs and
beneficiaries. These attorney fees usually require court approval as
to their applicability and reasonableness. Extraordinary fees can and
often do exceed the statutory commissions.

Contingent fees to attorneys are permitted when it is necessary to
institute claims and litigation by the estate against nonbeneficiaries.
Typical examples are claims for wrongful death, accidental injury,
breach of contract, and professional malpractice. Contingent fees
approximate one-third of any amount recovered by the estate. These
fees are set either by state law or by established practices of the bar
association.

Unless you, as executor, maintain some supervision and
control, attorney fees can get quite out of hand. Attorneys are not
noted for their self-discipline on fee matters. Next to taxes, attorney
fees are the highest single factor depleting an estate.

Your own fee as executor also is deductible. However, you are limited by the amount stipulated in the decedent's will. If the will is silent on this matter, you are limited by the statutory commission for the state of probate jurisdiction. You can apply for extraordinary fees and you can certainly deduct all direct expenses that you incur on behalf of the estate.

Chances are, all attorney fees will not be known by the time you file the Form 706. Recognizing this, there is a small-print line on Schedule J which reads: *amount estimated/agreed upon/paid*. This is your cue that said fees can be estimated and still be deducted. The same applies to your compensation as executor.

All Form 706's are audit examined by the IRS as standard procedure. This can be beneficial. It means that you have until the 706 is examined to make final payment on attorney fees and executor compensation.

Other Administration Expenses

Tax Regulation 20.2053-3(a) is particularly pertinent at this point. It is headed: **Deduction for expenses of administering estate.** It states in part that—

The amounts deductible from a decedent's gross estate as "administration expenses" . . . are limited to such expenses as are actually and necessarily incurred in the administration of the decedent's estate; that is, in the collection of assets, payment of debts, and distribution of property to the persons entitled to it. Expenditures not essential to the proper settlement of the estate, but incurred for the individual benefit of the heirs, legatees, or devisees, may not be taken as deductions.

Several important principles evolve from this regulation. If you master these principles, you can virtually eliminate any hassles on the final examination of your Form 706. And, you'll be able to take maximum advantage of the deductions you are allowed.

The important principles are:

One. The priority expenses allowed are those associated with property subject to claims. (Recall in Figure 8.1 that this is property in the estate owned directly by the decedent.)

Two. To be allowed, an expense must be *actually paid and necessarily incurred.* (Estimates — except for attorneys and executors — and personal-benefit expenses are not deductible.)

Three. The expenses must associate with the collection, appraisal, and protection of those direct assets of the estate. (Related property interests such as trust assets, life estates, and joint interests bear their own share of expenses.)

Four. The expenses must associate with the payment of debts and claims against the estate, and against the property which is to be distributed as directed by the decedent's will. (Expenses incurred by discretionary acts of the executor and by personal preferences of beneficiaries are not deductible.)

There is a whole gamut of legitimately deductible administration expenses. These include court costs, clerk fees, certification fees, recording fees, executor expenses, secretarial costs, photocopy fees, telephone charges, appraisal fees, accountant fees, tax preparation costs, caretaker fees, investment advice (for "parking" of liquid assets pending distribution), and *limited* travel expenses (if necessarily incurred in the performance of a duty).

Also deductible are those expenses necessary for securing and maintaining the property until distributed. Outlays for additions or improvements are not deductible. Except for protective repairs, storage costs, and ordinary maintenance, the expenses must associate with keeping the property in its initial state at time of decedent's death.

Where living animals are part of the decedent's estate, the cost of their feeding and care (pending assignment of final custody) are deductible.

The cost of feeding and care of the decedent's spouse, children, or other family members is *not* deductible. While a "family allowance" from the estate may be granted, it is treated as a partial distribution of the estate. Family support is not an expense of administration.

Necessary Selling Expenses

Selling property out of the estate generates questions about the deductibility of the selling expenses. There is a fine line between whether the sale is necessary, or whether it is an expediency.

Suppose, for example, that the decedent's will directed that his personal residence go to his daughter. The daughter is married and has a home of her own. She tells the executor that she has no use for the residence; she prefers the proceeds instead. The executor honors her preference and effects the sale. Is such sale "necessary"?

The answer is "No."

Where a decedent's will directs that a specific item of property be distributed to a specific beneficiary, the sale of that item — ordinarily — is a breach of executor duty. Although an executor has wide discretionary powers, these powers can only be used as necessary for carrying out the express wishes of the decedent.

To be a "necessary sale," it must be the only alternative for:

(a) the payment of taxes,
(b) the payment of other expenses,
(c) the payment of debts, and/or
(d) effecting distribution of the property.

Taxes, expenses, and debts are priority claims against an estate. By law, they take precedence over the distribution rights of beneficiaries. If the decedent's assets are of such form that there is insufficient liquidity to pay these priority claims, there is no alternative but to sell selected items of property. Such items should be those whose proceeds will be sufficient to cover the claims.

If selected items of property are sold, and all priority claims paid, the estate could be left with an "undistributable" illiquid asset. For example, a decedent with no surviving spouse or children, left his personal residence to seven of his distant nephews and nieces. It is quite impractical — and most unreasonable — to retitle a vacant residence into seven separate names, each of whom may live in a different legal jurisdiction. A sale in this case would be necessary for equitable and efficient distribution of the property.

Once necessary, all expenses for selling property are deductible. These expenses include sales commissions, auctioneer commissions, brokerage commissions, advertising and listing expenses, inspection fees, redemption fees, prepayment penalties, title transfers, settlement costs, and so on.

Debts of the Decedent

Everyone is expected to pay his legitimate debts. Death does not relieve one of this responsibility. If one's total assets in his estate are insufficient to cover his debts and expenses of administration, he is said to have a "bankrupt estate." As executor thereof, you must proceed through bankruptcy court to have your decedent's unsatisfied debts discharged. Otherwise, all debts must be paid . . . and are deductible.

Three basic principles concerning the deductibility of debts apply. These are:

One. The debt must represent a personal obligation of the decedent at the time of his death. (Debts occurring after death are expenses of administration.)

Two. Only those debts which are enforceable against the estate under local law apply. (If a debt is not legally enforceable, even though gratuitously assumed by the decedent, it is not deductible.)

Three. Contractual liabilities (payments over time) are deductible only to the extent that they were contracted bona fide, for adequate and full consideration in money or money's worth.

The essence of the above is that the decedent himself must have been a debtor at the time of his death. Debts of his spouse, his children, or his beneficiaries, even though they pledge as collateral their share of the assets of the estate, are not deductible. In community property states, since only one-half of the property is includible in the decedent's gross estate, only one-half of the debts against that property are deductible.

Credit-card charges, utility bills, promissory notes, medical bills, food bills: anything and everything due and owing at time of death, are deductible. This includes debts incurred but not yet billed, such as last illness expenses, last purchases made, charitable pledges, and the like. Interest due on past debts and late payment penalties also are deductible.

Unmatured and contingent debts are deductible, if it were reasonable to expect full payment if the decedent had not died. For example, suppose the decedent was a co-signer/guarantor of a bank loan to his son. Just before death, the son defaulted and made no further payments. The unpaid balance on principal plus accrued interest would be a debt of the decedent.

Consider the situation where the decedent was divorced at time of death. He was making court-ordered alimony payments and support payments for his minor children. The court-ordered payments for child support would be a deductible debt until each child reached legal age. The alimony payments would be deductible only to the extent that they could be actuarially determined. The amount of "alimony debt" would be based on the *lesser of* the ex-spouse's expectancy of remarriage, or ordinary life expectancy if remarriage is unlikely. Before any debt can be deducted, its amount must be determinable. There can be no indefinite or uncertain debt.

All deaths are publicly noticed. This means that creditors-in-the-woodwork are on notice to file their claims with the executor of the estate. If a creditor fails to file a claim for indebtedness within four months of public notification, it is not deductible. If a creditor files a claim for less than the full amount of debt, only the lesser amount is deductible. Once an estate is settled, any valid claims filed thereafter cannot be deducted.

In the case of marital debts, where both spouses enjoyed the benefits of indebtedness, only one-half of the debt can be deducted. If, however, it can be established that it was the decedent spouse who preponderantly enjoyed the benefits, then the full debt may be deducted. But do use caution. State laws differ markedly on the deductibility of marital/community/joint debts.

Mortgages, Liens, and Taxes

As to unpaid mortgages at time of death, Regulation 20.2053-7 is very clear. It declares specifically that—

A deduction is allowed from a decedent's gross estate of the full unpaid amount of a mortgage upon, or of any other indebtedness in respect of, any property of the gross estate, including interest which had accrued thereon to the date of death, provided the value of the property, undiminished by the amount of the mortgage or indebtedness, is included in the value of the gross estate.

In other words, if the decedent has a piece of property valued at $100,000 in his estate, and a 30-year mortgage on that property of $80,000, the entire $80,000 would be deductible.

Instead of $80,000, suppose there were two mortgages (a "first" and a "second") totaling $120,000, would the $120,000 be deductible?

The answer is "Yes." Provided, of course, that the two mortgages were bona fide and not the consequence of collusion, fraud, or misrepresentation.

If the mortgaged property is transferred in contemplation of death, say, into a "family trust," and the mortgage debt remains an obligation of the decedent, is it deductible? "No," if the property is not included in his estate. "Yes," if the property is included.

The situation is the same for any liens against property in the estate. There can be mechanics liens, creditor liens, utility liens, assessment liens, judgment liens, and others. To be deductible, the liens must be entered in the official records of the situs jurisdiction over the property. Threatened liens and contested liens do not count.

Unpaid taxes always are a form of lien. They are a statutory obligation which requires no official recording. Except for death taxes, all unpaid taxes at time of death are deductible. The most important are property taxes and income taxes. Unpaid sales taxes, excise taxes, and gift taxes also are deductible. Because, most frequently, death occurs between statutory due dates for taxes, the unpaid amount must be computed proportionately. This includes associated penalties and interest.

Special deduction care is required for mortgages, liens, and taxes owed jointly with the decedent and one or more survivors. Only the decedent's *allocable share* is deductible. However, if 100% of the property value is in the gross estate, then the total indebtedness can be deducted. In the case of husband and wife at time of one spouse's death, federal tax law directs that 50% (of value and debt) be allocable to each spouse.

Losses During Administration

The term "during administration" means the period of time from date of death to date of settlement of the estate. Typically, this period may span six to 18 months, though nine months is the ideal target time. You have nine months to file Form 706. Thereafter, unless you apply for an extension, the estate can be closed.

During the period of administration, if certain losses occur, the *net loss* is deductible from the gross estate. The "net" means the excess loss after compensation for insurance or otherwise.

A loss deduction may be taken only for those losses arising from fire, storm, shipwreck, or other casualty, or theft (including embezzlement). A "casualty" is a sudden, unforeseen event: not the deterioration or breakdown to property due to age, use, and lack of maintenance. Ordinary loss in market value does not count. The deductible losses must arise strictly from a casualty or theft.

If a casualty or theft occurs to any property in the gross estate, describe in detail the loss sustained and the cause. Attach "proof of loss." Identify the property for which you are claiming the loss by indicating the particular schedule and item number where the property is listed on Form 706. If you receive, or expect to receive, insurance or other compensation, so state the amount. This will reduce the amount of your net loss.

Net losses during administration are recorded, described, and valued on Schedule L ("L" for losses?) on Form 706. This schedule has two parts, namely:

Part I — Net losses during administration
Part II — Expenses not subject to claims.

Expenses Not Subject to Claims

In essence, property not subject to claims is that which is includible in the gross estate for tax accounting purposes, but which is not owned directly by the decedent. He is the beneficial owner only. We tried to explain this back in Figure 8.1. We are repeating it here for elaboration.

The "not subject to claims" phrase means the property cannot be attached — or litigated against — for debts, encumbrances, and personal obligations of the decedent. As such, the property assets cannot be pledged as collateral by the decedent. In addition, the property is not subject to the probative process under local law.

The most forthright example of property not subject to claims is that which is in a testamentary trust established by a predecedent of the decedent. Similar protected property may exist in a pension trust, an annuity trust, or a life insurance trust. The trusteed property is protected against claims for obligations of the decedent.

The requirement for deduction of expenses for "protected property" are more stringent than for property subject to claims. These requirements are:

(1) Expenses must be of the kind allowed, as if the property were subject to claims.

(2) Expenses are limited to those necessary for settling the decedent's interest in the property, and vesting good title in the beneficiaries.

(3) Expenses must be *diligently allocated* between those benefiting the decedent and those benefiting the beneficiaries of the protected property.

Expenses not subject to claims are itemized on Schedule L of Form 706. The official heading on this schedule is: **Net Losses During Administration and Expenses Incurred in Administering Property Not Subject to Claims.** Whew!

If Schedule L is applicable in your case, you are instructed to list the names and addresses of the persons to whom each expense was payable and the nature of the expense. Then you are to identify the property for which the expense was incurred by indicating the schedule and item number where the property is included in the gross estate. Obviously, if the not-subject property is not included in the estate, no administration expenses therewith are allowed.

Charitable and Public Bequests

All of the above matters are classed generally as "expenses of administration." They are addressed in the tax code by Section 2053: **Expenses, indebtedness, and taxes.** Every estate will have expenses of administration. All of these expenses are paid out of the estate checking account (of course). Recall Figure 2.3. For intermediate summary purposes, we present Figure 8.2 for "all decedent" estates.

A completely separate category of deductions is charitable and public bequests. Not every estate has provisions for charitable donations. Large estates often do because the amounts donated are fully deductible. Small estates sometimes do. To be valid deductions, the transfers to charity and/or public purposes must be within the testamentary power of the decedent, and the amount transferred must be ascertainable.

The conditions for deductibility of charitable bequests are prescribed in Section 2055. This section is headed: **Transfers for public, charitable, and religious uses.** The regulations thereunder are more clear than the tax code section.

Regulation 20.2055-1(a)(2) states the general rule for deductibility. It reads in part as—

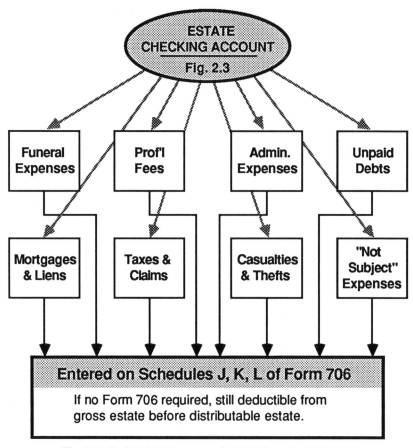

Fig. 8.2 - Deductible Expenses by "All Decedent" Estates

A deduction is allowed . . . from the gross estate of a decedent . . . for the value of property included in the decedent's gross estate and transferred by the decedent during his lifetime or by will—
To or for the use of any . . . [entity] . . . organized and operated exclusively for religious, charitable, scientific, literary, or educational purposes (including the encouragement of art and the prevention of cruelty to children or animals).

The charitable bequest must be directed to an *entity* and not to any private individual. There are no restrictions on the kind of entity (public, private, fraternal, veterans) to which the transfers may be made, so long as the entity does not engage in *prohibited transactions.* Prohibited transactions are those in which an entity official derives personal gain; the entity engages in propaganda; the entity attempts to influence legislation; and the entity officials deviate from the *exclusively charitable* role.

The decedent can direct only that property to charity over which he has clear testamentary control. He cannot bequeath someone else's property, nor that in which he holds only beneficial enjoyment. If he has joint ownership or fractional ownership interest in property, it cannot be claimed as a charitable deduction unless his interest can be separated and partitioned out. Not only must the property be deliverable to a charitable entity, its value must be ascertainable. Valueless property provides no deduction benefit.

One of the nice features of charitable bequests is that the decedent does not have to identify a particular charitable entity. He may grant his executor discretionary powers for selection of the entity or entities. The decedent must leave no doubt as to the charitable nature of his intentions. He must impose an obligation on his executor in such a way that the intended property cannot be diverted to noncharitable uses.

To claim the charitable deduction, Schedule O must be used. This schedule (**Charitable, Public, and Similar Gifts and Bequests**) asks several questions. In addition, the instructions insist that documentary proof be attached.

Adjustments to Charitable Bequests

Attaching documentary proof is not all. As executor, you have to show that the total property in the decedent's estate is sufficient to cover the charitable bequests after all prior bequests, deductions — and taxes — have been made. In other words, the amount claimed as a charitable deduction cannot exceed the *residual* estate: "its rest, residue, and remainder." This matter is frequently overlooked by nonprofessional executors.

Bequests to qualified charitable entities are not federally taxed. However, many states (and most foreign countries) do levy a "succession" tax on transfers to charity. The succession tax is higher on transfers out-of-state than on transfers within-state. This tax is not paid by the charity, but is paid by the decedent's estate. Consequently, by removing charitable property from the estate, the taxable assets remaining bear a higher proportion of taxes than otherwise would be their proper share.

Fortunately, there is remedy available: Section 2053(d)(1)(A). This subsection provides, in part, that—

*The value of the taxable estate may be determined, **if the executor so elects** . . . by deducting from the value of the gross estate the amount . . . of any estate, succession, legacy, or inheritance tax imposed by* [any state or foreign country] *upon a transfer by the decedent for public, charitable, or religious uses.* [Emphasis added.]

Note the emphasized phrase: "if the executor so elects." You have an election here because you have a choice between reducing the taxable estate by the amount of succession tax, or reducing the amount of the charitable bequest by the amount of succession tax. Reducing the taxable estate is often preferred. You make your election by including the succession tax on Schedule K (Debts of the Decedent, Etc.).

You also have another remedy for softening the disproportionate tax on noncharitable beneficiaries. It is Section 2055(c): Death Taxes Payable Out of (Charitable) Bequests.

If so instructed in the decedent's will, or if allowed under local law, you can apportion the federal death tax to the charitable bequests, and *reduce* such bequests by the amount of such taxes.

The apportionment ratio is:

$$\frac{\text{Value of charitable bequests}}{\text{Value of taxable estate before charitable deduction}} \times \text{federal death tax}$$

Make the computation on an attachment to Schedule O. Separate lines thereon instruct you to subtract the apportioned federal death tax from the property interests designated for charity. In this manner, other beneficiaries of the estate are not overpaying their proper share of taxes.

Why Deductions Important

If there were no deductions against a decedent's gross estate, his gross estate would become his taxable estate. The taxable estate is also the *taxable amount*. The taxable amount is the figure which is used to enter the death tax tables for computing the amount of tax. It's not quite this simple, but this is the general idea.

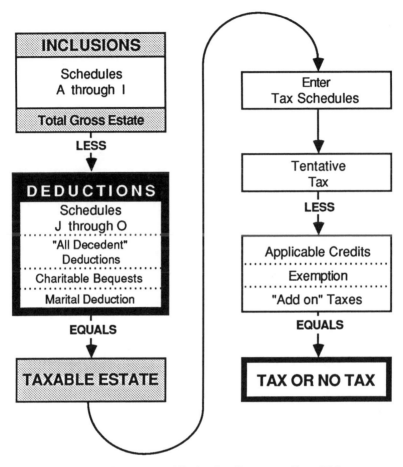

Fig. 8.3 - Sequence of Deduction Events on Form 706

With deductions, the taxable estate is reduced below that of the gross estate. This means that you enter the tax schedules at a lower figure than the gross estate. As executor, you obviously want to get the taxable estate (taxable amount) down as low as possible.

Getting the taxable estate down as low as possible is the focus of this chapter. For doing so, we have discussed the deduction schedules J, K, L, and O in some detail. The J-K-L schedules apply to just about every decedent. It is for this reason that we class J-K-L as the "all decedent" deductions. We emphasized this feature by means of Figure 8.2. We have added Schedule O (Charitable

Bequests) because many decedents — though not all — do make bequests to charitable and public organizations. Many do this throughout their income producing years, and continue the practice at death.

We have intentionally not addressed Schedule N (the ESOP Deduction) in this chapter. The main reason is that not many decedents are eligible: certain corporate-executive retirees, but few others. The "also" reason is that it is a transitional deduction which has now expired.

There is one very powerful deduction that we are reserving for the next chapter. This is the Marital Deduction: Schedule M. As its name implies, it is applicable only to spouses who are married at time of death of one spouse, thus leaving a surviving spouse to receive the bequest. If used wisely, this one deduction alone can reduce the taxable estate of a decedent to zero.

To help you sense where we are heading, we present Figure 8.3. Note that we have highlighted the deductions as a major phase intermediate between gross estate and final tax. Also note that before you get to the "final tax" — designated in Figure 8.3 as TAX OR NO TAX — there are other intermediate steps to pursue. One of these is the statutory exemption credit.

We have not yet told you one very important fact. For taxable estates of $600,000 or less, there is no death tax! Although Form 706 is required for gross estates of $600,000 or more, there is no death tax until the taxable estate itself exceeds $600,000. This figure is the *per decedent, per lifetime* exemption equivalent. We'll have more to say on this exemption in the next two chapters.

Now you know why the deductions discussed in this chapter are so important. Regardless of the amount of gross estate, if you can get the taxable estate down to $600,000 or below, the federal death tax is zero. Such would be the case, for example, for a gross estate of $750,000 with allowable deductions of $150,000 [$750,000 - $150,000 = $600,000 = zero tax].

9

THE MARITAL DEDUCTION

Misconceptions Surround The (Virtually Unlimited) Marital Deduction. If Not Used Judiciously, It Can Cause Loss Of The Decedent's $600,000 Exemption. There Is Only One Marital Deduction: Not Two. To Qualify, The Property Interests Must Be In The Decedent's Gross Estate. Such Property Must "Pass To" His Surviving Spouse . . . For Inclusion In Her Gross Estate. Debts Of The Decedent, Expenses of Administration, And Death Taxes Can Reduce The Net Value Of Property To The Spouse. A "Charitable Remainder Trust" Permits The Decedent To Get The Marital Deduction, And The Spouse To Get A Charitable Deduction.

A very special deduction against the gross estate of a decedent is the marital deduction. If legally married at time of death, and if other conditions are met, the marital deduction is unlimited in amount. This means that the taxable estate of the decedent could be reduced to zero, by this one deduction alone.

If claimed overzealously, the marital deduction creates severe tax problems for the survivor. Also, it can cause complete loss of the statutory exemption credit for the decedent. Every decedent is allowed a $600,000 exemption credit.

For example, suppose the decedent has a taxable estate of $600,000 before the marital deduction. He bequeaths the entire $600,000 to his wife, thereby reducing his taxable estate to zero. What happens to this $600,000 exemption credit?

It is totally lost!

Losing a $600,000 death tax exemption, because of overzealous marital deducting is not the most judicious estate tax planning. Worse yet, the $600,000 marital bequest could cost the surviving spouse $192,800 in taxes upon her death. Hence, there are many ramifications to the marital deduction which are not self-evident.

One Deduction Only

There is just one marital deduction per married couple. It is applicable to the estate of whichever spouse deceases first. If the husband dies first, his estate gets the deduction. If the wife dies first, her estate gets the deduction. Only one of the spousal estates gets it.

The marital deduction is a one-time, one-sum deduction. The spouses cannot agree between themselves (while alive) to split the deduction in such a way that the estate of each gets a fractional part. For example, any spousal agreement to allocate, say, 65% of the deduction to the wife and 35% to the husband is void. There is a special reason for this.

The marital deduction, as a concept, is based on one simple premise. If a deduction, called: *deductible interest*, is taken from one spouse's estate, it becomes automatically an **includible interest** in the surviving spouse's estate. From a tax theory point of view, one offsets the other. That is, the tax loss from the first decedent spouse is made up by a tax gain in the survivor's estate.

Let us exemplify. Suppose the marital interest at stake is $100,000. The husband dies first. His estate deducts $100,000, whereupon there is a corresponding tax loss. However, the $100,000 is includible in the surviving spouse's estate, such that when she dies her estate is $100,000 greater than it would have been otherwise. So, there is tax gain on her estate.

This deduction-inclusion offset is the very reason why the marital deduction applies only to married persons. There is no escapement of tax; it is simply shifted from one spouse to the other. There must be a surviving spouse for the concept to work. Persons who are divorced or unmarried at time of death are unaffected.

An attempt to portray the impact of this deduction-inclusion concept is presented in Figure 9.1. If the two spousal gross estates are equal before one spouse dies, they will be quite unequal after one dies. The challenge is to retain at least as much as $600,000 in each spouse's taxable estate.

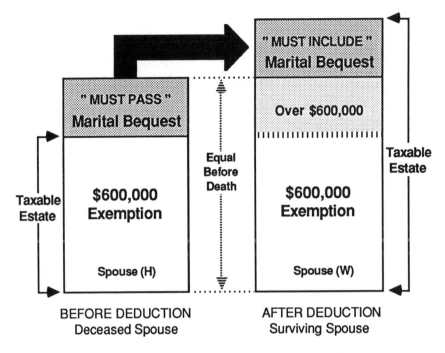

Fig. 9.1 - Depiction of "Deduction - Inclusion" of Marital Bequests

What happens if there is a simultaneous death, or "common disaster" as it is called?

As executor, first you have to look at both decedents' wills, and see what declaratory presumptions are made. If the wills are silent as to which spouse is presumed to have preceded the other, then you have to look at local law. If local law ascribes to the Uniform Simultaneous Death Act, and there is no sufficient evidence that the spouses died other than simultaneously (such as in an airplane or auto accident), neither is considered to have survived. Thus, for estate administration purposes, no marital deduction would be allowed. The tax effect on each would be as though the spouses were never married. There is no "deduction-inclusion" to be concerned about.

The Simultaneous Death Act allows a testator (will writer) to *presume* that he or she predeceased his or her spouse. This presumption of first-death can be particularly beneficial in separate property states, where the two spouses have greatly differing taxable estates. The spouse with the larger gross estate can presume that he or she dies first, and thereby make a marital bequest to help equalize the two death estates. In community property states, however, the first-death presumption has little value. Both spouses are already presumed to have equal taxable estates at time of (simultaneous) death.

The Statutory Wording

It is appropriate, at this point, to quote the general rule for allowance of the marital deduction. It is set forth in Section 2056 of the tax code: **Bequests, etc., to surviving spouse.** Subsection (a) thereof reads as follows:

*The value of the taxable estate shall, except as limited by subsection (b), be determined by **deducting** from the value of the gross estate an amount equal to **the value of any interest in property** which **passes or has passed** from the decedent to his surviving spouse, but only to the extent that such interest is included in determining the value of the gross estate.* [Emphasis added.]

Particularly note the emphasized phrase: "the value of any interest in property." No specific amount is specified. The deductible interest can be of any value. It is (virtually) unlimited. There are some limitations which we'll mention later.

But also note the phrase: "which passes or has passed from the decedent to his surviving spouse." This is the tax wording for embracing the deduction-inclusion concept described above. Of course, if there is a sufficient span of time between the death of the two spouses, some of the deducted amount could be consumed. If so, the amount consumed would diminish the includible tax effect on the survivor's estate.

Note also the phrase: "the taxable estate *shall* . . . be determined by deducting." This is mandatory wording. It means that if the decedent's will bequeaths certain property interests to his surviving spouse, as executor you have no choice but to deduct it. You have to claim the marital deduction in full, even though you know the tax effect on the surviving spouse's estate will be exacerbated. You cannot intervene with your after-death judgment to direct some of the maritally bequeathed property to other heirs and beneficiaries.

In large estates, the decedent's will may employ what is called a *formula bequest* to his surviving spouse. The purpose of such a bequest is to permit the executor some discretionary flexibility in arranging the best tax-spread between the two spouses. To permit this discretion, the formula instructions have to be quite clear.

Exemption Credit (Against Tax)

Another tax code feature you should know about is Section 2010: **Unified credit against estate tax**. This section reads in part as—

A credit of $192,800 shall be allowed to the estate of every decedent against the tax imposed.

Without explaining the conversion process at this time, be informed that a credit of $192,800 is equivalent to a $600,000 exemption against a decedent's taxable estate. (We'll show you the computations on this in the next chapter.)

Note particularly the phrase: "shall be allowed to the estate of *every decedent*." This means every spouse on his or her own. Thus, a married couple is allowed — in effect — *two* exemptions: one his, one hers. This was one of the messages in Figure 9.1.

For death years 1987 and thereafter, the per decedent exemption is $600,000 of taxable estate equivalent. This is quite a tidy death tax exemption. It means that if one spouse's taxable estate is exactly $600,000, his bottom-line tax is zero. This is so, with or without the marital deduction.

Asking a previous question again: What happens to the exemption credit if the taxable estate, by virtue of the marital deduction, is reduced to zero?

Answer: It is lost . . . completely! It is not refundable; it is not carryoverable from one spouse to the next.

Subsection 2010(d) makes this point very clear, namely:

The amount of the credit allowed by subsection (a) shall not exceed the amount of tax imposed.

If the tax imposed (after allowance for all deductions, including the marital deduction) is zero, the allowable exemption is also zero. If the tax imposed is greater than zero but less than the exemption amount, the unused credit portion is lost. Subsection 2010(d) applies to every decedent independently of his/her marital status.

A Dilemma Is Created

Confusion readily arises between the respective roles of the marital deduction and the exemption credit. The marital deduction applies only to the estate of the first spouse to become deceased. That spouse also is entitled to an exemption credit. The marital deduction applies to the gross estate to arrive at a taxable estate. The exemption credit applies to the tentative tax on the taxable estate to arrive at the net tax imposed. To help you visualize the sequential roles of these two items, we present Figure 9.2. Particularly note that the marital deduction "A" has to be taken before the exemption credit "B."

The marital deduction versus exemption credit creates a dilemma for the estate of the first decedent spouse. If his taxable estate (after the marital deduction) is less than $600,000, he loses entirely the difference between the exemption credit and his taxable estate. How can he retain the full exemption credit, and at the same time take advantage of the marital deduction?

There is no simple, straightforward answer. Much depends on the magnitude of the decedent's gross estate. Much depends on the amount of foreplanning by the decedent before death. And much depends on the executorial flexibility set forth in the decedent's will. As executor, your challenge is to preserve as much of the exemption credit as possible, within the bounds of the marital bequests assigned.

Ordinarily, one should take all the deductions he can against the gross estate. This way, the taxable estate is reduced . . . and so is the ultimate tax. However, when one deduction by itself (such as the marital deduction) can reduce the taxable estate to zero, caution is required. A zero taxable estate denies any benefit of the exemption credit. This suggests that, as executor, your first consideration is to estimate the decedent's taxable estate before barging ahead with the marital deduction.

Qualifications Required

Once you have ascertained that there is at least some taxable estate for the decedent, you can go forward trying to take maximum

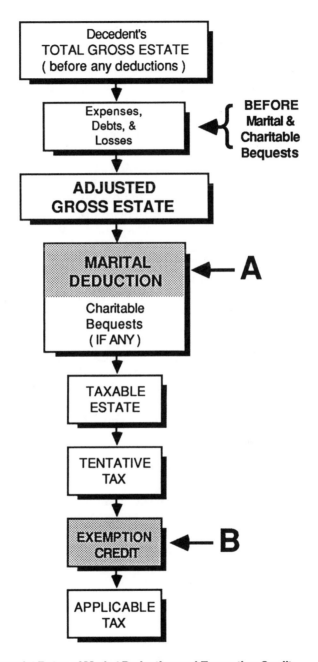

Fig. 9.2 - Sequential Roles of Marital Deduction and Exemption Credit

advantage of the marital deduction. To do so legitimately, you need to be sure of certain qualifying requirements.

To be allowed the marital deduction, the decedent must have been a U.S. citizen or resident at the time of his/her death. Furthermore, the deduction is allowable only if the decedent and the person to whom it passes are legally married at time of death. Being "legally married" means under the laws of the state in which the decedent dies. If he was in the process of divorce, and the divorce is not final at death, he is married. If a divorce is final before death, and the decedent has not rewritten his will to accommodate this fact, he is not married. If the decedent was divorced in one state, remarried in a second state, and died in a third state, he may or may not be legally married. It depends on whether the state of death recognizes the divorce/remarriage of the prior states.

For the marital deduction property to pass, the decedent's spouse must have survived him sufficiently long for the legality of the bequest to take place. This may be a few hours or a few months, depending on the mental capacity of the surviving spouse. If the surviving spouse is in a coma, or in a state of shock, or medically sedated, or otherwise mentally incompetent, she may not have the legal capacity to accept the property bequeathed to her.

To be deductible by the decedent, the maritally bequeathed property must be included on Schedules A through I (the asset schedules) of Form 706 for the decedent. As we tried to depict in Figure 9.2, marital deduction is removed from the decedent's adjusted gross estate. If the designated property is not included on the A through I schedules of the decedent, it is not a maritally deductible item.

And one final (practical) qualifying note. The residual estate of the decedent, whether taxable or not, must be sufficient to defray all expenses, debts, taxes, losses, and claims against the decedent and his estate. That is, property allowed as a marital deduction cannot deplete the gross estate to the point where administration and settlement costs cannot be met. It is for this reason that the marital deduction schedule (M) follows the schedule for expenses (J), debts (K), and losses (L) on Form 706.

Schedule "M" Bequests

The marital deduction property is claimed on Schedule M (the "M" for "married"?). This schedule carries the official heading: **Bequests, Etc. to Surviving Spouse**. The term "bequests" refers to the specific property interests prescribed by the decedent in his will. The term "etc." refers to those property interests which pass to the surviving spouse outside of the decedent's will. These are items for which an election is made by someone other than the decedent, but are included in his gross estate for tax accounting purposes.

The official instructions to Schedule M say—

You may list . . . only those items that the surviving spouse takes:
1.   *As the decedent's legatee, devisee, heir, or donee;*
2.   *As the decedent's surviving tenant by the entirety or joint tenant;*
3.   *As an appointee under the decedent's exercise of a power or as a taker in default at the decedent's nonexercise of a power;*
4.   *As a beneficiary of insurance on the decedent's life;*
5.   *As the surviving spouse taking under dower or curtesy (or similar statutory interest); and*
6.   *As a transferee of a transfer made by the decedent at any time.*

The instructions go on further to say that—

You should not list on Schedule M:
(a)   *The value of any property that does not pass from the decedent to the surviving spouse.*
(b)   *Property interests that are not included in the decedent's gross estate.*
(c)   *The full value of a property interest for which a deduction was claimed on Schedules J through L. The value of the property interest should be reduced by the deductions claimed with respect to it.*
(d)   *The full value of a property interest that passes to the surviving spouse subject to a mortgage or other encumbrance or an obligation of the surviving spouse. Include on Schedule M only the net value of the interest after reducing it by the amount of the mortgage or other debt.*
(e)   *Nondeductible terminable interests (unless a valid Q/TIP election is made).*
(f)   *Any property interests disclaimed by the surviving spouse.*

Sensitive to the prospects of a double deduction for disclaimed property, a headnote question appears on Schedule M. It reads as follows:

Did any property pass to the surviving spouse as the result of a qualified disclaimer? ☐ *Yes,* ☐ *No. If "Yes," attach a copy of the written disclaimer required by Section 2518(b).*

Section 2056(b) Limitations

As we have indicated previously, the marital deduction is a powerful tool for virtually eliminating any death tax to the first spouse who becomes deceased. But, contrary to general impressions, it is not an unlimited deduction. Certain statutory limitations are prescribed. These are found in Section 2056(b): *Limitation in the case of life estate or other terminable interest.*

Section 2056(b), a subsection in itself, has nine sub-subsections. For handy reference and identification, we list the nine subsections in Figure 9.3. Note that we show the complete subtitle to each subsection. We also list — in highly abbreviated form — the item(s) covered in each subsection. The sole purpose of Figure 9.3 is to counter any misconceptions that you might have, that the marital deduction is automatically unlimited. It is not.

There is one central idea behind Section 2056(b). The idea is to restrict an executor from claiming the marital deduction in those situations where predeath arrangements have been made outside of the decedent's will. Such arrangements are made with the intent of taking care of one's surviving spouse for life. Upon death of the surviving spouse, the property interests go to other beneficiaries predesignated by the decedent . . . or by his predecedent. These arrangements are called "bypass" bequests. They are intended to bypass the surviving spouse's estate, and thereby reduce her death tax.

Typical bypass arrangements involve marital trusts, endowments, annuities, gifts, reversionary loans, life insurance, life estates, terminable interests, and other contractual forms.

The target characteristics of property interests subject to the Section 2056(b) limitations are life estates and terminable interests. The general rule thereon reads, in part—

INTERNAL REVENUE CODE		
Sec. 2056 : Bequests, Etc., to Surviving Spouse		
Subsec. (b) :	Limitations in the Case of Life Estate or Other Terminable Interest	
Para.	**Subtitle**	**Item(s) Covered**
(b) (1)	General Rule : no deduction if -	Lapse of time, occurrence of event, or other contingency.
(b) (2)	Interest in unidentified assets.	Proceeds or assets with prior claims.
(b) (3)	Interest of spouse conditional on survival for limited period.	Common disaster deaths within 6 months.
(b) (4)	Valuation of interest passing to surviving spouse	Effect of death, inheritance, and succession taxes on net value.
(b) (5)	Life estate with power of appointment in surviving spouse.	Power to appoint entire interest or specific portion thereof.
(b) (6)	Life insurance or annuity payments with power of appointment in surviving spouse.	Power re proceeds of insurance, endowment, or annuity.
(b) (7)	Election with respect to life estate for surviving spouse.	Qualfied terminable interest property with income for life.
(b) (8)	Special rule for charitable remainder trusts.	Annuity trusts or unitrusts where spouse is the only noncharitable beneficiary.
(b) (9)	Denial of double deduction.	Only one deduction of any property interest per decedent.

Fig. 9.3 - Statutory Items that Limit the Marital Deduction

> *Where, on the lapse of time, or on the occurrence of an event or contingency, or on the failure of an event or contingency to occur, an interest passing to the surviving spouse will terminate or fail, no deduction shall be allowed . . .*
> *(A)* *if an interest in such property passes or has passed . . . to any person other than [the] surviving spouse; and*
> *(B)* *if . . . such person (or his heirs or assigns) may possess or enjoy any part of such property . . .; or*
> *(C)* *if such interest is to be acquired for the surviving spouse, pursuant to directions of the decedent, by his executor or by the trustee of a trust.*

The whole idea here is to rule out — as a marital deduction — those property arrangements in the decedent's estate plan which seek to avoid or minimize the "second" death tax, by bypassing the surviving spouse's estate.

Power-of-Appointment Exceptions

Section 2056(b) is referred to as the "terminable interest disallowance rule." As with all such rules, there are exceptions. Where the bypass arrangements give the surviving spouse broad power of appointment, the property subject to appointment can qualify for the marital deduction. The reason for this is that the appointed property is includible in the surviving spouse's estate (for second tax purposes) whether the marital deduction is claimed or not.

Every bypass arrangement does not have as its goal the avoidance or minimization of the second death tax. In some situations, the decedent is more concerned with the financial competency of the surviving spouse. If the decedent feels that his spouse would be a spendthrift, or an easy touch for aggressive children and salespersons, or is likely to remarry, he will set up certain safeguards for the management and conservation of his estate. He may provide these safeguards through life income, marital trusts, and insurance-type contracts, including endowments and annuities.

If the surviving spouse is given income for life with power of appointment into the bypass arrangement(s), she has economic control but not testamentary control over the decedent's estate. Economic control over a property interest by the surviving spouse is sufficient for claiming a marital deduction from the decedent's estate.

There are five requirements for obtaining the marital deduction for power-of-appointment property interests. These requirements are—

One. The surviving spouse must be entitled for life to all of the income from the entire interest or from a specific portion of the entire interest, or to a specific portion of all the income from the entire interest.

Two. The income must be payable annually or at more frequent intervals.

Three. The surviving spouse must have the power to appoint the entire interest (or specific portion) free of the trust or contract to either herself or to her estate.

Four. The power in the surviving spouse must be exercisable by her alone and (whether exercisable by will or during life) must be exercisable in all events.

Five. No person other than the surviving spouse may have a power of appointment over the interest or the specific portion enabling him to appoint any part to any person other than the surviving spouse.

Often, when a decedent prepares (and revises) his estate plan, including his will, the circumstances surrounding his estate and the estate of his spouse are known and calculable. At that time, direct bequests to the surviving spouse for marital deduction purposes may not be the best overall two-tax plan. With power-of-appointment arrangements, the decedent's executor and surviving spouse are given the benefit of hindsight. This is particularly true of Section 2044 property with the Q/TIP election. This was discussed in Chapter 7, and pictorialized in Figure 7.1.

Charitable Remainder Trusts

There is one truly unique exception to the terminable interest disallowance rule. It pertains to charitable remainder trusts.

A charitable remainder trust is an arrangement whereby the decedent gives his spouse an income interest for life, with the remainder of his estate going to charity upon her death. He gets a marital deduction from his estate; she gets a charitable deduction from her estate. Any double death tax is avoided altogether!

There are two forms of charitable remainder trusts: annuity trust and unitrust. An annuity trust pays to the spouse a *specified sum* which is at least 5% of the *initial* value of all property placed in the trust. A unitrust pays to the spouse a *fixed percentage* which is at least 5% of the *annual* value of all property in the trust. In both of these trust forms, the obligation to make payments to the decedent's spouse begins on date of death of the decedent. The trust arrangements can be set up either before death or at death.

The trust instruments establishing the charitable remainder arrangements must be clear and specific. There must be no power to invade the principal of the trust for other than the spouse and charity. The spouse must be the only noncharitable beneficiary. Payments must be made to the spouse at least annually. The payments must be made for a term of years (not more than 20) or for the life of the spouse. When the spouse deceases, the *entire remainder* (not just a fraction or specific assets) must go to a qualified charity or for charitable uses.

A special rule permits all assets designated into a (qualified) charitable remainder trust to be claimed as a marital deduction on the decedent's Form 706. This rule is Section 2056(b)(8)(A). It reads in part as—

If the surviving spouse of the decedent is the only noncharitable beneficiary of a qualified charitable remainder trust, paragraph (1) [the general disallowance rule] *shall not apply to any interest in such trust which passes or has passed from the decedent to such surviving spouse.*

As an executor, therefore, your duty is to ascertain if a charitable remainder trust has been (or is to be) set up. If so, is it tax qualified? You may need expert legal assistance to examine, or to prepare, the proper trust instruments.

Completing Schedule M

For a married decedent, Schedule M will (most probably) constitute the largest single category of deductions on the entire Form 706. As such, you should expect this schedule to be examined very closely by tax agents. Make each entry thereon clear and specific. Cross reference each entry to the exact item or items on the asset schedules. Do Schedule M right and, chances are, other schedules will not be examined so closely.

Schedule M	BEQUESTS , ETC. TO SURVIVING SPOUSE		Form 706
Item No.	Description	Estate Value	Net Value
1.	50% interest in personal residence (652 W. Elm St.) described in Sch.A at item 3 - - - - - - - - - - - - - - - - - LESS 50% mortgage (Allyear Savings) on Sch. K at item 5 - - - - - - - - - - -	116,000 (36,280)	79,720
2.	Trust deed on 40 Ac. unimproved land, held in name of decedent alone but subject to community property; On Sch. C at item 4 - - - - - - - - - - - - LESS 50% community property - - - - -	65,280 (32,640)	32,640
3.	All proceeds of Forever Life Policy No. 6429820, for 10 years certain; On Sch. D at item 1 - - - - - - - - - - - - - LESS loans outstanding, as per Form 712, No.6 - - - - - - - - - - - - - -	100,000 (56,314)	43,686
4.	All assets in Power of Appointment Trust with Briggs Bank as Trustee, consisting solely of C/D's, T/D's, and M/M accounts; On Sch. H at item 1 - - - - - - LESS unpaid trustee fees and administrative expenses - - - - - - - - -	201,640 (8,962)	192,678
5.	A pecuniary bequest of $350,000 as designated in Paragraph Eight of decedents Will ("in-kind") ● Cash available in estate - - - - - ● 10 Ac. of improved land, on Sch. A at item 4 as $185,000. (revised appraisal attached) - - - ● All items 1 through 5 (stock) on Sch. B which total $115,000. (revised appraisal attached) - - -	65,000 200,000 85,000	350,000
	TOTAL BEQUEST (before tax effect)		698,724

Fig. 9.4 - Examples of the Specificity Required on Schedule M

The official instructions for completing Schedule M say—

List each property interest included in the gross estate which passes from the decedent to the surviving spouse and for which a marital deduction is allowed. Number each item in sequence and describe each item in detail. Describe the instrument (including any clause or paragraph number) or provision of law under which each item passed to the surviving spouse. If possible, show where each item appears (number and schedules) on Schedules A through I. Enter the value of each interest before taking into account the Federal estate tax or any other death tax.

Some examples of the specificity required on Schedule M are presented in Figure 9.4. Note that we have listed five separate items. Each is an attempt to portray the "net value" of the bequeathed item, using information already on Form 706. It is the **net value** which passes: not the gross. Otherwise, the decedent would get the effect of a double deduction: one deduction for the gross value, and — separately — another deduction for allocable loans, debts, and expenses.

We particularly call your attention to Item 5 in Figure 9.4. It uses the term "pecuniary bequest" (pecuniary means: measure in money). A *pecuniary bequest* is the assignment of a specific dollar amount in cash or "in kind." This permits the substitution of property interests for money. The bequest may also be a specific percentage of the decedent's distributable estate, again in kind. Thus, the decedent leaves it up to his executor as to how the pecuniary bequest may be fulfilled.

There can be many months between the date of decedent's death and the date of fulfillment of his pecuniary bequest. During this period, some of the property may increase in value and some may decrease in value. Which valuation date — date of death or date of precuniary distribution — does the executor use to fulfill the bequest?

In this situation, the executor must distribute cash and property "fairly representative" (or having an "aggregate fair market value") of the appreciation and depreciation *of all property* in the estate at the time of the pecuniary distribution. This means that the pecuniary property has to be reappraised as of the date of its passing to the surviving spouse.

10

DEATH TAX COMPUTATION

Not Every Decedent Will Pay A Federal Death Tax.
Much Depends On His Marital Status, "Taxable Estate,"
Adjusted Taxable Gifts, The Unified (Exemption) Credit,
And Other Applicable Credits That Might Apply. For
Married Decedents, The Surviving Spouse (Upon Her/His
Demise) Almost Invariably Will Pay Death Tax. There
Also Are Two "Add-On" Taxes: Generation-Skipping
And Excess Retirement Accumulations. If Extension Of
Time To File Or Pay Is Required, Application Is Made On
Form 4768.

Not every decedent will pay a federal death tax. Much depends
on his marital status and on the amount of his taxable estate (gross
less deductions).

As we have seen in the previous chapter, a married decedent
who bequeaths his entire (distributable) estate to his surviving
spouse may pay no tax at all. His surviving spouse (now single)
will pay tax if her taxable estate exceeds $600,000. If the surviving
spouse — or any other decedent — has a taxable estate of less than
$600,000, there will be no tax.

There is no such thing as a joint death tax return, as there is a
joint income tax return. This is so whether death occurs to the two
spouses one at a time, or to both simultaneously. For tax
computation purposes, death severs a marriage and reverts the
spouses to single persons. As a consequence, there is just *one* tax
rate schedule. It applies to all decedents, regardless of marital or
family status.

Tax Rates Start High

When it comes to the subject of taxes, most persons think in terms of income taxes. They pay income taxes every year of their productive life. Consequently, they tend to think of tax rates and tax dollars in income tax terms. They get used to certain rates and dollars, and think that similar rates and dollars apply in death. This is one reason why death tax planning is not taken too seriously during life.

There is a dramatic difference between income taxes and death taxes. The subject of death taxes is an entirely different league from that of income taxes.

Whereas income tax rates start at 15%, death tax rates *start* at 37%!

Whereas for ordinary taxpayers income taxable amounts range up to about $100,000, death taxable amounts start at the $600,000 mark!

The complete (federal) death tax rate schedule is presented in Figure 10.1. Note that the first two columns say amount subject to *tentative tax*. This is amount of tax *before credits*. The exemption credit and other credits reduce the applicable tax below the tentative tax.

Note in Figure 10.1 that the 37% rate applies to estate amounts of $500,000 to $750,000. We have highlighted this bracket amount in the figure. We said above that the death tax rates start at 37%. The more complete (and correct) statement is that death tax rates start at 37% *after* allowance for a decedent's exemption credit. The maximum taxable estate exemption is $600,000. So, indeed, applicable death taxes do start at 37%. The rates extend up to 55% where the actual death tax can exceed well over $1,000,000.

As executor, before you can use the tax rate schedule in Figure 10.1, two separate summaries must be prepared. Summary 1 is the total gross estate (Schedules A through I); Summary 2 is the total allowable deductions (Schedules J through O). Both summaries are detailed on Form 706 under the heading of "Recapitulation." (Recall Figure 6.2.) Both summaries are required whether any death tax is ultimately due or not.

Summaries 1 and 2 bring you to the stage of establishing the decedent's taxable estate. That is:

AMOUNT SUBJECT TO TENTATIVE TAX		Tax on Amount in Column A	Tax Rate on Excess Over Col. A
Amount Exceeding	But Not Exceeding	$ [Before Credits]	%
Col. A	Col. B	Col. C	Col. D
10,000	20,000	1,800	20
20,000	40,000	3,800	22
40,000	60,000	8,200	24
60,000	80,000	13,000	26
80,000	100,000	18,200	28
100,000	150,000	23,800	30
150,000	250,000	38,800	32
250,000	500,000	70,800	34
500,000	750,000	155,800	37
750,000	1,000,000	248,300	39
1,000,000	1,250,000	345,800	41
1,250,000	1,500,000	448,300	43
1,500,000	2,000,000	555,800	45
2,000,000	2,500,000	780,800	49
2,500,000	3,000,000	1,025,800	53
3,000,000	——	1,290,800	55

Fig. 10.1 - The Federal Death Tax (Unified) Rate Schedule

Summary 1: Total gross estate $_____
Summary 2: Total allowable deductions (_____)
Taxable estate (subtract 2 from 1) $_____

But you are still not yet ready to enter the tax rate schedule in Figure 10.1. You have to *add* to the taxable estate, the decedent's "adjusted taxable gifts." Let us explain.

Adjusted Taxable Gifts

One of the "sleepers" in the death taxation process is that certain gifts during life are tax reviewed at death. Because gifting during life can reduce taxes at death, there arose the concept of a *unified* gift-death tax rate schedule. This unified concept went into effect on December 31, 1976.

Up until that date, the gift tax rates and exemptions differed from those for death taxes. This led to much computational confusion, as gifts were usually accelerated in contemplation of death.

Prior to December 31, 1976, the gift tax exemption was $30,000 (per donor). The death tax exemption was $60,000 (per decedent). In 1976, the two were unified into one exemption of $47,000 phased-in through 1981. In 1982, the unified exemption was again increased.

Because of the unification of gift taxes with death taxes, certain "adjustments" to a decedent's taxable estate have to be made. These adjustments necessitate that all gifts during the life of a decedent be classified into three time periods. These periods are:

- Gifts before 1977
- Gifts after 1976 and before 1982
- Gifts after 1981

By definition, a *taxable gift* is the amount of gift after an "annual exclusion" is applied. Before 1977 the annual exclusion was $3,000. After 1981 the annual exclusion was increased to $10,000. After 1976 and before 1982, the $3,000 annual exclusion was complicated by the phase-in of the unified exemption credit.

The net effect of the above is that all gifts made by a decedent after December 31, 1976 are swept into a special category called "adjusted taxable gifts." The exception to this sweep-in rule is those gifts which are within three years of death and includible in the gross estate (via Schedule G: Transfers During Decedent's Life). Consequently, the term *adjusted taxable gifts* includes those made after 1976 and before three years before death.

Suppose, for example, a decedent gave $53,000 to his son in 1978 and $60,000 to his daughter in 1982. He died in 1986. What are his adjusted taxable gifts?

Answer: $100,000. That is, the sum of $53,000 less $3,000 ($50,000) in 1978, and $60,000 less $10,000 ($50,000) in 1982. [The $3,000 and $10,000 are the annual exclusions, above mentiond.] Any gifts made in 1983 (part year), 1984, 1985, and 1986 (part year) would be automatically included in his gross estate.

This feature — adjusted taxable gifts — drives home the point that gifts once made are not thereafter tax forgotten. They are resurrected at death and **added** to the decedent's taxable estate. This is to avoid any possible "double exemption" on the same dollar amount: one exemption at time of gift and another exemption at time of death.

Before you tackle the computations for "adjusted taxable gifts," we urge you to read thoroughly the separate instruction pamphlet to Form 706. This pamphlet provides a Worksheet TG ("TG" is Taxable Gifts) for reconciling the decedent's *lifetime* taxable gifts, if any. You are instructed—

You must obtain all of the decedent's gift tax returns (Form 709) Before you complete Worksheet TG.

Good luck!

Examples of "Tentative Tax"

As executor, once you have resurrected the adjusted taxable gifts, you are in a position to enter the (gift-death) tax rate schedule and extract the decedent's tentative tax. The sequential procedure for doing so is as follows:

Step 1 — Total gross estate (Summary 1)
Step 2 — Total allowable deductions (Summary 2)
Step 3 — Taxable estate (Subtract 2 from 1)
Step 4 — Adjusted taxable gifts (Resurrections)
Step 5 — Adjusted taxable estate (*Add* 3 and 4)
Step 6 — Tentative tax (Unified rate schedule: Fig. 10.1)

Three numerical examples will help illustrate the computation procedures and fine points involved.

Example 1. Your decedent's gross estate is $500,000. He has a $100,000 mortgage on his home and $50,000 in other debts. In 1988, he made a $10,000 gift to his only nephew. He died in 1991 (just over 3 years after making the gift). What is his tentative tax?

Answer 1. Step 1 — $500,000
Step 2 — 150,000
Step 3 — 350,000
Step 4 — Zero (no taxable gift because in 1988 the annual exclusion was $10,000)
Step 5 — 350,000
Step 6 — $104,800 (*Tentative* tax)

Example 2. Your decedent's gross estate is $1,000,000. His total allowable deductions (including a marital deduction of $250,000) are $350,000. His adjusted taxable gifts are $150,000 (after annual exclusions). All gifts were made before three years before death. What is his tentative tax?

Answer 2. Step 1 — $1,000,000
Step 2 —   350,000
Step 3 —   650,000
Step 4 —   150,000
Step 5 —   800,000
Step 6 — $ 267,800 (*Tentative* tax)

Example 3. Your decedent has a gross estate of $3,000,000. He has a marital deduction of $600,000; a charitable deduction of $100,000; and other allowable deductions amounting to $150,000. He made a series of taxable gifts (after exclusions) as follows:

1978 — $ 50,000
1980 —   75,000
1984 —   100,000
1989 —   100,000

He died in 1991 (within 3 years of the 1989 gift). What is his tentative tax?

Answer 3. Step 1 — $3,000,000
Step 2 —   850,000
Step 3 — 2,150,000
Step 4 —   225,000 (the 1989 gift is already included in Step 1)
Step 5 — 2,375,000
Step 6 — $ 964,550 (*Tentative* tax)

As you can sense from these examples, once a decedent's gross estate exceeds $500,000, his tentative tax increases rather dramatically. Also, when a gross estate exceeds $1,000,000, gifting plays an increasing role in death tax planning. For these and higher estates, you must make a determined effort to resurrect all gifts made by the decedent after December 31, 1976 . . . and before three years before death.

The Unified (Exemption) Credit

Previously, we have used the terms "exemption credit" and "exemption equivalent." Technically, these are not official gift-death tax terms. We used them at the time to avoid a premature discussion on the *unified credit*. This credit is a direct offset (reduction) against the tentative tax. It produces the effect of an exemption. The unified credit applies to every decedent.

The specific amount of credit is prescribed in the tax code as Section 2010: Unified Credit Against Estate Tax. Although quoted previously in Chapter 9, we are requoting Section 2010 here for emphasis. This section reads in pertinent part as follows—

A credit of $192,800 shall be allowed to the estate of every decedent against the tax imposed . . . [in Figure 10.1].

A "credit" is a dollar-for-dollar tax offset. It is the authorized tax dollar reduction, after taking into account the tax rate percentage corresponding to the decedent's adjusted taxable estate. The credit of $192,800 corresponds to an equivalent taxable estate of $600,000. This is the amount that we referred to previously as a flat-out "exemption." This equivalence comes from working Figure 10.1 "backwards."

Let's check this out.

Enter Figure 10.1 at the shaded row: $500,000 — $750,000. The tax dollar amount corresponding to a taxable estate of $600,000 is—

155,800 + 0.37 x (600,000 - 500,000) =
155,800 + 37,000 = $192,800

A decedent's "applicable tax" follows *after* the exemption credit is applied. In other words, we subtract the unified credit of

$192,800 directly from the tentative tax to arrive at the applicable tax.

Using the three examples outlined in steps above, the corresponding applicable taxes would be:

Example 1:	Tentative tax	=	104,800
	Unified credit	=	(192,800)
	Applicable tax	=	$ Zero
Example 2:	Tentative tax	=	267,800
	Unified credit	=	(192,800)
	Applicable tax	=	$ 75,000
Example 3:	Tentative tax	=	964,500
	Unified credit	=	(192,800)
	Applicable tax	=	$771,700

Sequence to "Applicable Tax"

Unfortunately, we have introduced a situation where the more comprehensible term "applicable tax" has no official standing. The technically correct and proper term is "Adjusted estate tax (not less than zero): Balance due." Getting from the tentative tax to the "balance due" tax is not the one-step process that we illustrated above. It is a 20-step process!

The term "tentative tax" is official. It is indicated as step 6 on page 1 of Form 706 under the portion labeled: Tax Computation. Following step 6, there are steps 7 through 26. These 20 steps all deal with "adjustments" to — and for — various credits and "add-ons," including the unified (gift-death) credit. The official line numbers (steps) on Form 706 are presented in Figure 10.2. We have edited the official designations for better clarity.

Steps (lines) 7 through 12 in Figure 10.2 deal with adjustments for prior gift taxes paid and to the unified credit itself. From the tentative tax (step 6), reduction for any prior gift taxes paid is allowed. From the unified credit, any prior gift exemption credit that was taken is subtracted. Thence, step 12 becomes the "Adjusted estate tax (**not less than zero**)."

There is a special reason for the "not less than zero" instruction at step 12. At this point, if there is no tax, all other potentially applicable credits are lost. There is no provision on Form 706 for refundable tax credits as in the case of income tax.

Form 706	U.S. ESTATE TAX RETURN	Page 1
	Part 2 - Tax Computation	
1	Total gross estate	
2	Total allowable deductions	
3	Taxable estate (SUBTRACT line 2 from line 1)	
4	Adjusted taxable gifts (after 1976)	
5	ADD lines 3 and 4	
6	TENTATIVE TAX (on line 5 amount) ➔	
7	Amount of gift tax paid (on gifts in line 4)	
8	Gross estate tax (SUBTRACT line 7 from line 6)	
9	Unified credit against estate tax	
10	Adjustment to unified credit	
11	Allowable credit (SUBTRACT line 10 from line 9)	
12	SUBTRACT line 11 from line 8 (BUT NOT LESS THAN ZERO)	
13	Credit for state death taxes	
14	SUBTRACT line 13 from line 12	
15	Credit for gift taxes on pre-1977 gifts	
16	Credit for foreign death taxes	
17	Credit for tax on prior transfers	
18	ADD lines 15, 16, and 17	
19	NET ESTATE TAX (SUBTRACT line 18 from line 14) ➔	
20	Generation-skipping tax	
21	Tax on excess retirement accumulation	
22	TOTAL TRANSFER TAX (ADD lines 19, 20, and 21) ➔	
23	Prior payments, if any	
24	Treasury bonds redeemed for payment	
25	Total payments (ADD lines 23 and 24)	
26	BALANCE DUE (SUBTRACT line 25 from line 22)	

Fig. 10.2 - Official Steps on Form 706 for Computation of Tax

There are four other credits that may or may not be applicable to your decedent's estate. Even when applicable, they can be used only if there is a positive amount (greater than zero) at step 12.

In order of sequence, the other — possibly applicable — credits are:

(1) credit for state death taxes
(2) credit for federal taxes on pre-1977 gifts
(3) credit for foreign death taxes
(4) credit for tax on prior transfers

These credits follow step 12 above. They are "processed" via steps 13 through 18 in Figure 10.2. Of the four credits listed, two are fairly common. These are the credit for state death taxes and the credit for federal death tax on prior transfers to your decedent.

Credit for State Death Taxes

Virtually every state levies a death tax in some form. To minimize confusion in terminology with the federal estate (death) tax, the terms "inheritance" tax, "legacy" tax, and "succession" tax are used. These labels are simply another tax on the privilege of dying.

Built into the federal tax code is a maximum credit amount for death taxes paid to one or more state governments. If two or more state jurisdictions are involved — such as a decedent dying in one state with property in another state — prorata credit for each is allowable up to the maximum credit amount. The maximum credit is based on a fixed percentage of the federal taxable estate.

The federal tax code on point is Section 2011: **Credit for State death taxes.** Subsection 2011(a) thereunder reads in part:

The tax imposed by Section 2001 [Estate Tax] *shall be credited with the amount of any estate, inheritance, legacy, or succession taxes actually paid to any State or the District of Columbia, in respect of any property included in the gross estate* [of the decedent].

The maximum amount of credit is set forth in a lengthy schedule (20 different rates) incorporated in Section 2011(b). This credit schedule is also given in the official instructions accompanying Form 706, and so is not presented here. The credit rates range from a low of 0.8% for taxable estates of $100,000 to a high of 16% for taxable estates over $10,000,000.

As with all tax credits, there are certain "catches" involved. One catch is that the state credit amount is based on the federal taxable estate *reduced by $60,000*. This reduction often causes confusion when entering the state-credit rate schedule.

There is still another catch. Some states levy a tax on decedent transfers to public, charitable, and religious organizations. The federal does not tax these transfers. Hence, where there is a state death tax on charitable transfers, that portion of the state tax has to be "backed out" before claiming the federally allowed credit.

The credit is allowed only for those state death taxes actually paid. Because of sometimes many differences between state taxes and federal taxes, and because of conflicting jurisdictions when the decedent's property is located in more than one state, the total state death taxes are not always known when Form 706 is filed. In these circumstances, Section 2011(c) allows up to four years after the filing of Form 706 to claim the state death tax credit.

Many states deliberately structure their minimum death tax to match the maximum federal credit allowed. The rationale for doing so is that, up to at least the maximum federal credit, there is no additional tax burden on the decedent. He either pays it to the federal or to the state: not to both. Any state death tax beyond the maximum federal credit is, of course, a surtax burden.

To illustrate the role of the state death tax credit against the federal death tax, consider a decedent with a taxable estate of $800,000. Using figure 10.1 and the state credit tables in the instructions to Form 706, the following amounts unfold:

Tentative tax	= $267,800
Exemption credit	= (192,800)
Applicable tax	= 75,000
State credit	= (22,800)
Net federal tax	= $ 52,200

In other words, the executor pays $52,200 to the IRS **and** $22,800 to the inheritance tax authority of the state of domicile of the decedent. Altogether, the executor pays $75,000 which is the applicable federal tax, if there were no state death tax credit.

Credit for Tax on Prior Transfers

Sometimes a decedent may have — or will have — acquired property from other decedents, called: *decedent transferors*. These transferors may already have paid federal death tax on property transferred to your decedent. If this is the case, a credit (limited in amount) is allowed against your decedent's tax for prior taxes paid on the same property. The idea behind this credit is to reduce, in part, any double/triple tax on the same transferred property.

This credit — called the *decedent transferor credit* — is prescribed in Section 2013 of the tax code. This section is lengthy and complicated. But we will give you the gist of it.

To benefit from Section 2013, you must understand the role of "attributable property." This is the net value of transferred property from a prior decedent which is *directed* to your decedent. It is not essential that the designated property actually be in your decedent's estate at time of his death. It is essential, however, that you be able to identify the property in the decedent transferor's estate. Its "net value" is the designated property less prorata adjustments for deductions, credits, and taxes of the prior decedent.

As you should suspect, computation of the credit is not straightforward. For this computation, a special 35-line worksheet is provided in the separate instruction pamphlet to Form 706: Worksheet for Schedule Q — Credit for Tax on Prior Transfers. The bottom line on this worksheet is an *attributable tax* paid by an eligible decedent transferor. This attributable tax is the maximum credit possible.

The allowable credit depends on the intervening years between dates of death: the transferor and your decedent. Section 2013(a) prescribes the allowable credits as—

100% if transferor died within 2 years *after* decedent
100% if transferor died within 2 years *before* decedent
 80% if transferor died within 3rd and 4th years before decedent
 60% if transferor died within 5th and 6th years before decedent
 40% if transferor died within 7th and 8th years before decedent
 20% if transferor died within 9th and 10th years before decedent

There is no limit to the number of eligible decedent transferors. If more than one, the computation becomes quite involved. A decedent transferor may himself be a transferee from a prior decedent. To help you visualize the potential complications involved, Figure 10.3 is presented. You should be aware that for each transferor indicated, you will need a copy of that decedent's Form 706. Obtaining the transferor Form 706's could become your downfall. No transferor Form 706: no transferor credit.

Do note in Figure 10.3 the 100% band: two years after *and* two years before your decedent's death. Surely, within this time frame

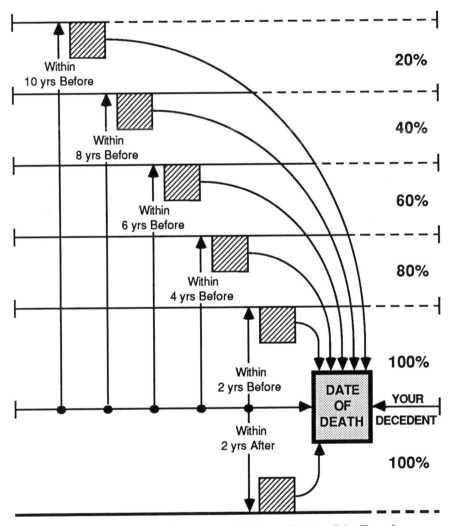

Fig. 10.3 - Eligible Credit Percentages for Taxes Paid on Prior Transfers

you can track down the records on any decedent transferor and get a copy of his Form 706. You may even be able to do this for the 80% transferor(s): that is, those within four years before your decedent's death. Except for a spousal transferor, the time and effort to locate other 706's and identify attributable properties may not be justified for transferors in the 60% and lower percentage bands. Hence, there is a practical limit to claiming the decedent transferor credit.

Two "Add-On" Taxes

After all applicable credits are subtracted (including credit for certain prior gift taxes paid: step 7 in Figure 10.2), we arrive at step 19: *Net estate tax*. Ordinarily, this would be the amount of death tax due. BUT, there are two potential "add-on" taxes that have to be considered.

The two potential add-ons are the generation-skipping tax (step 20) and tax on excess retirement accumulations (step 21). The mere mentioning of these taxes implies applicability to only quite large estates. Incidentally, these two add-ons are called *transfer* taxes, in keeping with the same rationale that the death tax is a transfer tax.

The generation-skipping transfer (GST) tax is computed by using Schedules R and R-1 in Form 706. The Schedule R is for tax payable by the decedent's estate; the Schedule R-1 is for tax payable by certain trusts includible in the decedent's estate. In general, the GST tax applies to estates of decedents dying after October 22, 1986.

We touched on the GST tax in Chapter 6, and referred you to Sections 2601 through 2663 of the Federal tax code. We also referred you to the separate instructions for Schedules R and R-1. Your focus of attention is on any and all grandchildren of the decedent who have been bequeathed sums of money in excess of $100,000. This means studying (again) the decedent's will, any trusts created by the decedent before his death, and any "direct skips" from one trust to another. If the total of all generation-skipping bequests exceeds $1,000,000, the GST tax applies . . . at the 55% rate. Unless you have a keen legal mind of your own, interpreting the tax ramifications of "grandchildren trusts" may require your seeking legal counsel.

The transfer tax on excess retirement accumulation (step 21) is not covered adequately in the Form 706 instructions. Therefore, you must resort to the small-print reference to Section 4980A of the tax code. Subsection 4980A(d) is particularly instructive. It reads in essential part—

> *The* [death] *tax imposed . . . with respect to the estate of any individual shall be increased by an amount equal to 15 percent of the individual's excess retirement accumulation.* [Emphasis added.]

The "excess retirement accumulation" is the amount by which the actuarial present value of the retirement plan exceeds the product of $150,000 times the statistical life expectancy of the decedent immediately before his death. This information has to be obtained from the chief actuary of the retirement plan administrator. Once this excess amount is known, the add-on tax is simply 15% of that amount.

We are now at step 22. This is the total transfer (death) tax in Figure 10-2. This is the sum of the net estate tax plus the add-ons, if any.

From the total death tax, you subtract any prepayments in the form of cash, assigned financial interests, and T-bond redemptions. This leaves a **balance due** as the very last entry in the death tax computation on Form 706.

Filings, Extensions, & Payments

Ordinarily, Form 706 is required to be filed, and the full tax paid, within nine months of your decedent's death. But as you can surmise from the above, this due date for filing/payment may not be reasonable in all cases. If, despite your best efforts, you are unable to complete Form 706 on time, what do you do?

Answer: You apply for an extension of time.

The tax code authorizes two separate kinds of extensions. One is an extension of time to *file* (Section 6081). The other is an extension of time to *pay* (Section 6161). The application for one of these extensions does not automatically include the other. Each must be applied for separately, and each must be approved separately. Approval, of course, is by the Internal Revenue Service.

A special form has been devised for death tax return extensions. It is Form 4768: **Application for Extension of Time to File U.S. Estate Tax Return and/or Pay Estate Tax.** As executor, it is your duty to prepare this form. You must do this sufficiently early to permit the IRS to consider the application and reply to you before the 9-months due date.

Approval of an extension of time to file will not exceed six months. Even for this length of time, you must establish good and sufficient cause why it is impossible or impracticable to otherwise complete the 706. Missing or insufficient information is not good enough. You can always make estimates, and correct them later if you have to.

You should always file Form 706, even if you cannot pay all of the tax at that time. You can apply for extension of time to pay based on *reasonable cause* and/or *undue hardship*. Reasonable cause includes insufficient liquid assets in the estate at time of filing, or that the assets are tied up in litigation, or that the assets are inaccessible because they have been consigned as collateral for loans. Undue hardship would be that liquidating the estate to pay tax would destroy a farming operation or family business, or that liquidation of other assets could only be done at a sacrifice price or in a depressed market.

In general, extensions of time to pay can be "automatically" approved for periods up to six months. However, there are two exceptions, namely: Sections 6163 and 6166. Section 6163 allows up to three years after termination of any prior interest(s) in specially designated assets (called "reversionary/remainder" property). Section 6166 allows up to five years for payment, for estates consisting largely of closely-held businesses and family farms.

Where approval for payment is granted beyond six months from the regular due date, a security bond has to be furnished. As executor, therefore, you have to arrange for posting of this bond. The necessary bonding expenses are part of the administration costs . . . allowable as a deduction on Schedule J (Form 706).

11

FIDUCIARY FORM 1041

After Form 706, If The Corpus Estate Generates Income Of $600 Or More, Form 1041 (Fiduciary Income Tax Return) Is Required. For Form 1041 Filings, A Separate Tax Identifying Number Is Used. This Causes Payer Confusion Between The Decedent's SSN And The Estate's EIN. Nevertheless, Income And Nonincome Assets Must Be Separated, And When Necessary Sales Are Made, Gain And Loss Computations Must Be Shown. All Ordinary Caretaking Expenses Are Allowed As Deductions. It Is Simpler To Pay Any Income Tax Due Out Of The Estate Rather Than Passing It Through To The Beneficiaries.

Altogether, there are *three* different federal tax returns that have to be filed, with respect to a decedent. There is a "final" Form 1040 to cover the decedent's tax accountable income while he was alive (in his death year). There is a death tax Form 706 for transferring marketable assets to the decedent's heirs and legatees. And there is a transitional Form 1041 to report the tax accountable income from the decedent's corpus (estate) from date of death to date of final distribution to the decedent's will-directed beneficiaries.

As executor, it is your duty to see that each of these three forms — **1040, 706,** and **1041** — are prepared and filed in a timely manner. You are required to sign each form and make full payment of tax (where due). There are also corresponding tax returns to be filed with the state of domicile of the decedent at time of death *and*, possibly, with the state of situs of his major realty holdings if such property is outside of his state of death. Fortunately, most states "piggyback" the federal returns. This should ease your task somewhat.

We addressed the final Form 1040 back in Chapter 4 (last section therein). We've discussed in some depth Form 706 in Chapters 6 through 10. Now, we want to direct this entire chapter to Form 1041. This form has some similarities to Form 1040, but it has major differences which you should know about. Form 1041, however, is an **income** tax return. If you keep this point in mind, you'll understand better why it is required.

The Fiduciary (Corpus) Estate

In various chapters previously, we have referenced the "date of death" of the decedent. For your duties as executor, the decedent's date of death is like a solid wall. It fixes and stops the inventorying process for determining the decedent's gross estate. The marketable assets of the decedent on that date form the basis for computing the amount of death tax. It is as though all of his assets were bundled up and sold on that date. We know, of course, that this does not happen.

After the date of death, there emerges an entirely new domain: a *corpus estate*. The corpus also has to be managed and accounted for. In some cases, there could be modest gain in the corpus. In most cases, however, there is significant diminution. Overall, the corpus estate has a short, finite existence. It extends from the date of death to final distribution to those beneficiaries named by the decedent. This differs from the gross estate . . . which is an instant-of-time affair.

The concept that we are dealing with here is important; so much so that a diagrammatic representation is needed. Accordingly, we present Figure 11.1. As should be self-evident therein, unless the entire gross estate were sold on the date of death (an impossibility), and placed into a noninterest-bearing account, some of the decedent's corpus assets could generate income. If — as is most probable — the corpus estate does indeed generate income, an entirely different tax accounting process is required. As intended in Figure 11.1, the corpus estate and fiduciary estate are one and the same. The term "corpus" refers to the decedent himself/herself, whereas the term "fiduciary" refers to **you** as caretaker of the decedent's estate.

Between the date of death and date of (final) distribution, there may be interest income, dividend income, rental income, royalty

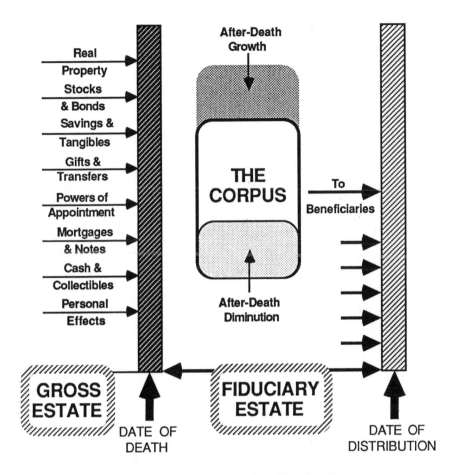

Fig. 11.1 - Domain and Duration of the Fiduciary Estate

income, residual business income, farm income, partnership income, capital gain (or loss) income, and other forms (such as income from other estates and trusts) which derive strictly from the corpus estate itself. If the "corpus income" is $600 or more, it has to be tax reported. For this, a completely separate return is required, namely: **Form 1041 — U.S. Fiduciary Income Tax Return.**

Whereas you sign Form 706 as the executor (of the gross estate), you sign Form 1041 as the *fiduciary* (of the corpus estate). Thus, without realizing it, you have taken on another responsibility: that of being a "trustee" for the property, money, and income of the decedent's estate. The instructions to Form 1041 define a fiduciary as—

The executor, executrix, administrator, administratrix, personal representative, or a person in possession of property of a decedent's estate.

The Form 1041 instructions go on to say that—

An estate of a deceased person is a taxable entity separate from the decedent. It generally continues to exist until the final distribution of the assets . . . are made to the heirs and other beneficiaries. The income earned . . . during the period of administration or settlement must be accounted for and reported.

Filing Date Confusion

Form 1041 is a calendar year return: January 1 through December 31. So, too, is Form 1040. Both returns have to be filed by April 15 following the close of the tax year. What happens in the death year?

Suppose your decedent dies on November 15. Do you file a final 1040 only? Do you file an initial 1041 only? Or, do you file both?

Answer: Unless a decedent dies exactly on December 31, technically, two separate forms are required: a 1040 **and** a 1041. The 1040 is for the living period of the death year; the 1041 is for the death period of the death year. Each is called a "short year" return, as each is less than a full 365 calendar days.

In a more practical vein, if a decedent dies on December 16 or thereafter, file a final 1040 only. On the other hand, if he dies on or before January 15, file an initial 1041 only. Short-year returns of 15 days or less are an exercise in futility.

Thus, if a decedent dies anytime on January 16 and thereafter, to December 15, *two* income tax returns are required for the death year: 1040 **and** 1041. This often leads to much confusion. We portray this confusion in Figure 11.2.

Confusion arises because of the necessity for *income allocation*. That is, the income generated during the death year must be allocated between a 1040 return (while living) and a 1041 return (after death). In most situations, this allocation is difficult . . . and exasperating.

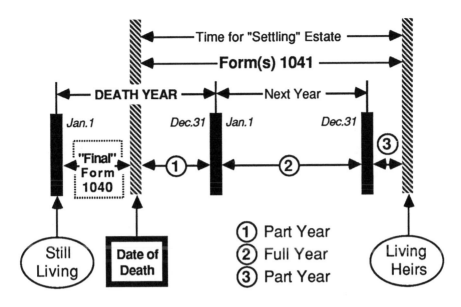

Fig. 11.2 - The Relationship of Forms 1040 and 1041

The first 1041 filed is called the "initial" return. The last one filed is called the "final" return. The Form 1041 itself has checkboxes for indicating which is which. As an executor, you will face the necessity for filing at least one Form 1041. This could be your "initial/final" return. More than likely, you will file two — and possibly three — Form 1041's before the corpus estate is distributed to all of the decedent's beneficiaries. This is the underlying message in Figure 11.2.

A point to keep in mind is that Form 1040 could be a joint return between the decedent and his/her surviving spouse. In this case, the surviving spouse files the 1040 on a regular calendar year basis, irrespective of the date of death. **There is no joint Form 1041.** Consequently, you and the surviving spouse have to coordinate carefully the year-of-death allocation matters.

Introduction to Form 1041

The key differences between Forms 1040 and 1041 show up immediately at the top of each form. In each case, the respective top blank spaces read—

Form 1040:

Name of individual_____
Social Security number_____ (SSN)

Form 1041:

Name of estate_____
Employer identification number_____ (EIN)

So, right off the bat, you are faced with having to enter a tax identifying number (EIN) which you do not have. Therefore, before filing your first Form 1041, you must apply for an EIN number. You cannot use the social security number of the decedent. If you trip up on this, we guarantee you endless computer matching headaches.

You apply for the EIN number on IRS **Form SS-4**: Application for Employer Identification Number. Don't let the word "employer" throw you. A fiduciary estate can employ persons during its transitional tenure.

Get Form SS-4 from your nearest IRS office, or have a tax preparer get one for you. On the top line of the SS-4, fill in the name of the decedent as—

Estate of John J. Jones, Deceased

. . . then enter his (not your) social security number.

Form SS-4 contains a number of blank spaces and check-boxes, most of which are not applicable. There are only two check-boxes of concern to you. They are—

Type of organization ☐ Other (specify) _____Estate_____
Reason for applying ☐ Other (specify) _____Form 1041_____

You sign and date the SS-4 form with your title as *Executor/Fiduciary*. Write your own address in the space provided. Within 15 to 30 days, you'll be assigned an EIN number.

While your application for EIN is in process, get hold of Form 1041 and its official instructions. While you may not want to prepare Form 1041 yourself, you should at least have a copy in your possession for familiarization purposes. It's quite different from Form 1040. You'll be signing it . . . "Under penalties of perjury."

Strictly for introductory purposes, we present in Figure 11.3 a highly edited and abridged arrangement of Form 1041. We are showing the front page only. There is a back page with several schedules thereon, and there are additional schedules which have to be attached, when applicable. Particularly note in Figure 11.3 the types of income reportable, and the types of deductions allowable. We'll touch on the highlights of each of these categories in a moment.

Two general comments at this time. Form 1041 has a space in its upper portion labeled: *Date entity created.* This, of course, is the date of death of your decedent. When you sign Form 1041 at the lower portion, there is a space labeled: *EIN of fiduciary.* You leave this EIN space blank. You, yourself, do not have an EIN. Nor do you need one. And, above all, do not enter your social security number here either. The EIN space in the signature block is for corporate and professional fiduciaries only. The EIN for the estate goes in the very first blank space at the top right-hand portion of Form 1041 (as emphasized in Figure 11.3).

Income Producing Assets

Keeping in mind that Form 1041 is an *income* tax return, it becomes necessary that you segregate all assets in the corpus (fiduciary) estate into two major groupings. One group consists of those assets which produce income; the second group, the nonincome assets. The nonincome assets would be such items as: (a) the decedent's personal residence, (b) raw land, (c) tangible personal property such as vehicles and equipment (not used in business), (d) collectibles and objects of art, (e) checking-only accounts, and (f) other miscellany of marketable value with no current income potential.

It is not your job as a fiduciary to rearrange the decedent's assets to produce income. Basically, you are a conservator and a disburser. You are not an entrepreneur seeking to maximize income from the corpus estate.

But, if, at the time of the decedent's death, there are some assets already producing income when you come on the scene, your job is to segregate those assets and let them continue generating income. At least until such time as you either have to liquidate them or transfer them directly to the distributees.

Form 1041	FIDUCIARY INCOME TAX RETURN	Calendar YEAR

Check Boxes	Name of Estate	EIN
☐ Estate	Name of Fiduciary	Date of Death
☐ Trust	Address of Fiduciary	No. of K-1's
☐ Initial	City, State, & Zip	▶ attached ___
☐ Amended		
☐ Final		

INCOME

1	Interest income	
2	Dividends from securities	
3	Income (loss) from partnerships / trusts	
4	Net rental / royalty income (loss)	
5	Net business / farm income	
6	Capital gain (loss) [ATTACH SCHED. D (1041)]	
7	Ordinary gain (loss) [ATTACH FORM 4797]	
8	Other income [STATE NATURE & SOURCE]	
9	Total Income (Add 1 through 8)	▶

DEDUCTIONS

10	Interest paid	
11	Taxes paid	
12	Fiduciary fees	
13	Charitable deduction	
14	Attorney, accountant, & preparer fees	
15	Other deductions [ATTACH SCHEDULE]	
16	Subtotal deductions (Add 10 through 15) ──▶	
17	Adjusted Total Income (Subtract 16 from 9) ▶	
18	Income distribution deduction [ATTACH K-1's]	
19	Estate tax deduction [ATTACH COMPUTATION]	
20	Statutory exemption	
21	Total Deductions (Add 18 through 20)	▶

TAX & PAYMENTS

22	TAXABLE INCOME (Subtract 21 from 17) ──▶	
	Tax from Tax Rate Schedule ──────▶	
	● Applicable credits ● Tax withheld ● Estimated prepayments } ADD ──▶	
	NET TAX DUE	▶

Signature Block	_____ (Fiduciary)	_____ (Date)

Fig.11.3 - Edited / Abridged Arrangement of Form 1041 (Page 1)

Typical income-producing assets in a corpus estate would be rental real estate, a small business (or a large one), royalties from oil and mineral property, farm and grazing land, securities generating dividends, interest-bearing accounts, and repayments (principal and interest) on personal loans, installment notes, and trust deeds. The income from all of these sources has to be systematically identified, recorded, and accumulated. Ultimately, this income — after allocable deductions — will be distributed to beneficiaries.

In Figure 11.3, there are eight categories of income-producing assets that, as applicable, must be identified on your Form 1041. Each applicable category requires a separate itemized schedule attached to the fiduciary form. In all cases but one (capital gains and losses), the attached schedules are virtually identical to those associated with Form 1040. Thus, your own familiarity with Form 1040 procedures can be helpful in keeping track of the decedent's corpus income.

When Assets Are Sold

In many cases, it becomes necessary to sell assets — income and nonincome alike — to convert the corpus estate into more convenient distributable form. The estate may need money to pay off debts, taxes, and expenses. Sometimes, there are destitute beneficiaries dependent entirely on the decedent, who need money to continue their lives. When the need arises, your duty as executor is to sell the appropriate assets and corral the money into the estate checking account.

When you sell any of the decedent's assets, you will have to confront Schedule D (Form 1041): **Capital Gains and Losses**. This itemization schedule is divided into five parts, namely:

Part I	—	Short-Term: Assets Held One Year or Less
Part II	—	Long-Term: Assets Held More Than One Year
Part III	—	Summary of Parts I and II
		(a) Beneficiaries
		(b) Fiduciary
		(c) Total
Part IV	—	Computation of Capital Loss Limitation
Part V	—	Computation of Capital Loss Carryovers
		A - Loss Carryover Limit
		B - Short-Term Loss Carryovers
		C - Long-Term Loss Carryovers

For purposes of short-term, long-term entries on Schedule D (Form 1041), the fiduciary holding period starts on the date of death of the decedent. The value at the date of death becomes the "cost or other basis, as adjusted" when an item is sold. This is why, back in Figure 5.4, even if the alternate valuation date was used for gross estate purposes, the value at date of death is simultaneously required. In other words, the values listed in the asset schedules of Form 706 become the tax basis in each item of property, when it is sold after death. One needs a "tax basis" in order to determine gain or loss at time of sale. Any expense of sale *adds* to the Form 706 tax basis.

We're not going further into Schedule D (1041), as you'd probably have a tax preparer do it for you. But if you want to do it yourself, there are official instructions that you can follow.

There is one key point to keep in mind, however. In Part III of the Schedule D, you have a choice to make. You can pass the net gains and losses directly through to the beneficiaries, OR, you can retain all or a portion of the gains and losses in the fiduciary accounting. Your choice would probably depend on how near you were to making final distribution of the estate to the designated beneficiaries.

Computer Matching "Nightmare"

We now have to tell you something that we really don't want to tell you. You won't believe it can happen to you . . . until it happens. You face a computer matching nightmare.

Big Brother, with its total reliance on computer-matching every financial transaction in America, has created a tax identifying monster. Every payer in the United States who pays you money, engages in barter, or makes a property exchange, MUST REPORT EVERY DOLLAR to the Internal Revenue Service (IRS). If a bank pays you $10 in interest, it is reported to the IRS. If you hold a security that pays $62 in dividends, the nominee broker reports it to the IRS. If you sell a parcel of raw land for $5,000, the title company reports it to the IRS. If an oil exploration company pays you $67.52 in royalties, the oil company reports it to the IRS. If a commercial tenant pays you $900 in rent, the tenant reports it to the IRS. If you cash in an insurance policy on the life of other than the decedent, the insurance company reports it to the IRS. And on and on this goes.

These payer reportings are called "information returns." Altogether, there are approximately 25 different payer information returns! They are derivatives of the Form 1099 series, the Form K-1 series, and the Form W-2 series. You are probably familiar with some of the 1099's, K-1's, and W-2's in your own 1040 experience. The situation is much worse when it comes to Form 1041.

For Form 1041 purposes, what tax reporting number do you think is used? Is it the decedent's social security number? Or, is it the estate's employer identification number?

Answer: The EIN of the estate.

But how does each payer know what your decedent's estate EIN is? The IRS will not inform them: it's not required to. So, guess who has to inform the payers?

YOU, the executor/fiduciary of the corpus estate. You have to inform each and every payer of money to the estate the EIN of the estate. It will get garbled. It will also get mixed up with the decedent's SSN which the payers were using before the decedent's death. All 1099's, K-1's, and W-2's are on a calendar year — not death year — basis. It's a nightmare. Believe us.

To help you visualize the problem that we are getting at, we present Figure 11.4. The problem lies mostly with the IRS. Because of its bureaucratic inertia, it takes 18 to 24 months after death before that agency and its master computer get around to cross-matching the information you report on Form 1041 with that reported to the IRS by your payers. We guarantee you that there will be foul-ups. There also will be mix-ups between the decedent's SSN and the estate's EIN. The problem is particularly atrocious for the year of death.

Certain Deductions Allowed

Any income producing entity (the corpus estate is an "entity") will incur ordinary and necessary expenses in connection with that income. There are certain management expenses and fees; there are legal and professional costs; there could be operating losses, casualties, and thefts; there could be interest on money borrowed, and maintenance and taxes on property held. And there could be other rather minor expenses, such as supplies, utilities, postage, some travel, and so on. All of these types of expenses are allowable deductions against the total income of the Form 1041 estate.

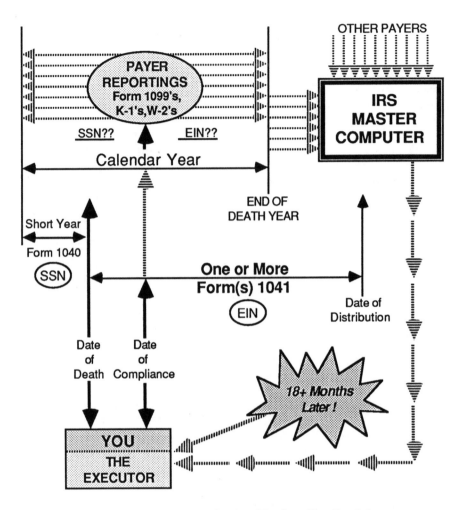

Fig. 11.4 - Why IRS's Computer Seldom Matches After Death Income

The specifically allowable categories of deductions are those identified as items 10 through 15 in Figure 11.3. Use caution and do not confuse these deductions with those allowable on Form 706 (Chapter 8) against the gross estate. The Form 1041 deductions relate to the corpus estate only: its management, care, and distribution. There are significant differences between the Form 1041 deductions and the Form 706 deductions.

For example, against the gross estate (Form 706), you can deduct all federal income taxes due from the decedent at time of his death. You cannot deduct any federal income tax against Form 1041. You can deduct state and local income taxes, but not federal. For debts not paid off from the gross estate, you can deduct on Form 1041 the interest incurred to pay off the death taxes, but not interest to pay off income taxes or personal debts of the decedent.

Why these differences?

Because, technically, the taxable gross estate for death tax purposes should be free of any ongoing debts, taxes, and expenses. What's left after death taxes — the corpus estate — starts a whole new system of operational expenses of its own. If the Form 706 tax accounting is done right, and is fully complete, there should be no possibility of duplicate-type expenses to deal with in the corpus estate. This is why we covered Form 706 in some detail before introducing you to Form 1041.

We can make our point with executor fees and fiduciary fees. You are allowed to deduct all of your executor fees and costs on Form 706. Separately, as manager of the corpus estate, you are also allowed reasonable fiduciary fees and costs on Form 1041.

Income Distribution Deduction

There is one special deduction allowable on Form 1041 which is *not* allowable on Form 706. This is the "Income Distribution Deduction." This one deduction alone could wipe out all of the federal (and state) income tax due on Form 1041.

The income distribution deduction is the aggregate of all income distributions that you make to the beneficiaries of the estate. That is, you are allowed to pass through to the beneficiaries any or all of the corpus income. Whatever amount you do pass through is deductible on Form 1041.

There's a simple reason for this deduction. Whatever amount of corpus income is passed through is income-taxed to the beneficiaries on their own Forms 1040. In other words, the income tax is paid either by the fiduciary (on Form 1041) or by the beneficiaries (on Forms 1040), or by both.

There is a 17-step procedure for computing the income distribution deduction. These 17 steps are set forth on the back of Form 1041. The accompanying instructions caution you also to prepare **Schedule K-1** (Form 1041): **Beneficiary's Share of Income,**

Deductions, Credits, Etc. You prepare a separate K-1 for *each* beneficiary.

In essence, then, if you intend to claim the income distribution deduction on Form 1041, you have to prepare an aggregate computational schedule and one or more distributive schedules (K-1's). This means affixing the name, address, and social security number to Schedule K-1 (1041) for each distributive beneficiary. The original copy of each K-1 is sent to the IRS. This means that you are an informant payer, "spying" for the government against each beneficiary of the decedent. (Figure 11.4 revisited.)

A dilemma faces you, which we depict in Figure 11.5. Do you really want to antagonize the decedent's heirs and legatees before you have settled the estate? Do you want to subject them to the possibility of a tax penalty for their misperceptions? Do you want to engage in much unnecessary paperwork for a duty lasting 9 to 15 months at most?

Our suggestion is this. Forego the income distribution deduction. Enter "None" in the applicable space on Form 1041. Then compute and pay all of the income tax out of the corpus estate.

Tax Computation and Payment

There is only one tax rate schedule for a Form 1041 entity. There are no single, married, or other filing status rate schedules, as there is for Form 1040. This fact alone simplifies the 1041 tax computation.

For familiarity purposes, the one tax rate schedule is approximately as follows:

$ 0	to	$ 5,000	at	15%
$ 5,000	to	$15,000	at	28%
$15,000	to	$30,000	at	33%
Above $30,000			at	28%

We say "approximately" because the bracket ranges change each year with inflation, and with fine tuning of the tax laws. We just wanted you to see that the rates are not as devastating as the death tax rates.

Before applying the Form 1041 tax rate schedule, you need to compute the taxable income of the corpus estate. The sequence for doing so is fairly self-evident in Figure 11.3. For most fiduciary

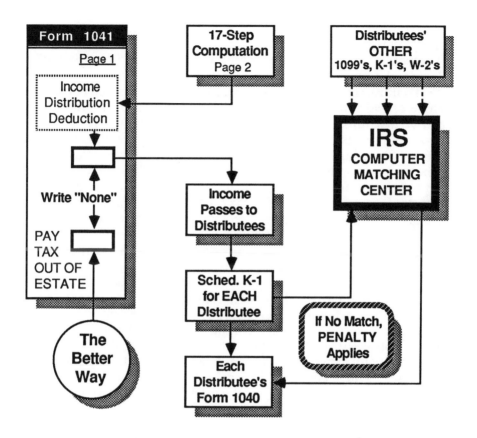

Fig. 11.5 - Form 1041 "Paperwork" for the Income Distribution Deduction

estates, seldom is there taxable income in excess of $30,000. The reason is that your fiduciary activities are a transitional phase in the tax process, during which the amount of taxable income tends to decline on its own.

In skimming down the sequence in Figure 11.3, you must have noticed the deduction at Line 19 that we haven't told you about. The "Estate tax deduction." What is this? you ask.

It is a deduction allowed by Section 691(c) of the tax code for . . . *income in respect of a decedent*. In other words, if the total income in Step 1 above includes income that was an obligation to the decedent personally, before his demise, and the income asset was included in the gross estate for Form 706 purposes, there is an allowance on Form 1041 for any "double tax" on the same income.

Determining the proportionate amount of double-tax is rather complicated. But you get the idea. IRS Regulation 1.691(c)-1 [Deduction for estate tax attributable to income in respect of a decedent] describes the computation in detail.

To illustrate the double-tax effect, consider an installment sale of property which the decedent made before his demise. There were to be five installments of $20,000 (principal and interest). He received two installments before his demise, thus leaving three installments ($60,000) owing him at time of death. These three installments were included in his gross estate for which he was death taxed. Yet, the same three installments are included in the fiduciary estate where they are income taxed. Double tax? For this, Section 691(c) allows a deduction on Form 1041 for a prorata share of the death tax paid.

Line 20 in Figure 11.3 shows a "statutory exemption." For fiduciary estates, the exemption amount is $600. This is allowed by Section 642(b) of the tax code. This is a "poor cousin" compromise for the $2,000 personal exemption that would have been allowed on Form 1040, had the decedent not deceased.

There are a few other computational features on Form 1041 which, unless you have very complex sources of corpus income, would not likely apply. At any rate, by following the form itself, you eventually arrive at the bottom line: TAX DUE. Whatever the amount is, write a check to "Internal Revenue Service" and include thereon the notation: EIN ___(of the estate)___, Form 1041 (year). You sign the check — and the return — as the fiduciary.

12

CLOSING MATTERS

Closing An Estate Is A Summarization Of the Transitional/Liquefying Role Of The Executorial Process. Essentially, An Intermediate Estate Called The "Fiduciary Estate" Is Created. After Taxes, Debts, And Expenses Are Paid, The Net Cash-On-Hand Plus Value Of Unsold Assets Constitute The Distributable Estate. At This Point, You File A "Petition For Final Distribution." After Notifying Distributees And Others, A "Final Judgment" Is Rendered. This Judgment Plus Acknowledgment Of Receipt Of Cash And/Or Property By Distributees Discharges Your Executorial Duties.

Estate administration cannot go on indefinitely. There comes a point in time where the estate must be closed, and the residual assets distributed to the "new owners" thereof. These are the heirs and legatees named in the will, and others named by the court.

Heirs are those persons who have a direct blood relationship with the decedent. They are persons only: not entities. They have certain state-law rights outside of the will, and for this reason they are priority distributees.

Legatees are those who do not have a blood relationship with the decedent, but they are provided for in the will by name. Legatees may be persons or entities (such as trusts, corporations, and charitable organizations). Their rights are limited to the terms of the will.

"Others" are appointees by the probate court after death of the decedent. Example appointees are trustees (for missing heirs), conservators, guardians, successor heirs (when the will-named heir deceases before distribution), the State Controller, and the like.

If the estate consists of property belonging to a missing heir who is never found, or is refused by an heir or legatee, or is property which cannot be transferred because of ambiguity in the will, what do you think happens to it?

Answer: It *escheats* (reverts) to the political state where the property is located. In other words, the distributee owner becomes the State Controller. We tell you this now so that you are fully aware that every estate can be closed: no matter what.

Preview of Closing

The typical span of time between date of death and date of closing (settling) an estate runs from six to twelve months. Estates with probative issues and/or those requiring the filing of Form 706 with extensions may take as long as 18 months. Back in Chapter 1 we targeted nine months. We did this to stimulate you into prompt action: otherwise, procrastination could set in. Realistically, you should be able to complete all estate affairs within one year of death.

Some states require statutory finalization within specified times after the date of issuance of letters testamentary. If not closed within these times, a report to the probate court is required. One such state is California. Its probate code Section 1220 reads verbatim as follows:

> *The personal representative* [executor] *shall either **petition for an order for final distribution** of the estate or make a report of status of administration not later than the following times:*
> *(a) In an estate for which a federal estate tax return is not required, within one year after the date of issuance of letters.*
> *(b) In an estate for which a federal estate tax return is required, within 18 months after the issuance of letters.*
> [Emphasis *not* added.]

As just cited, you have to file a *petition* for final distribution. We can hear you now. You are probably saying to yourself: "Good grief: another petition!"

Take heart. It is different in form and purpose from any other petition. It is a check-list type summary of everything that you have done, or were supposed to have done. From this summary, a *judgment* on final distribution is prepared. This judgment directs you to transfer specific items of property or specific amounts of money to specific distributees. The idea behind this petition and judgment is that all proper interests have been duly notified, and that they all have had opportunity for "their day in court." The estate is to be closed. Once closed, your legal liabilities are discharged and your personal liabilities cease.

The "Fiduciary Estate" and You

You may not identify the situation as such, but you are actually working with three separate estates. There is the decedent's gross estate: that which is on hand at time of death. There is the distributable estate: that which is on hand at closing and assignable to distributees. In between death and distribution, there is the *fiduciary estate*. The fiduciary estate is a transitory arrangement under your sole discretion and control. The term "fiduciary" means a relationship founded on trust and confidence. You will have to account for the fiduciary estate entrusted to you. This includes the filing of Form 1041 when income is generated.

The fiduciary estate undergoes substantial change from the decedent's form to the distributee's form. The change involves conversion, diminution, claims, exchanges, rearrangements, some income, and some losses. Administrative expenses and compensation for services have to be paid. Some assets have to be sold and converted to cash. Other assets have to be reassigned. In the process of all of this, there may be partial (preliminary) distributions to needy beneficiaries. There also may be fire, theft, damage, deterioration, and other "caretaker" matters to account for. Though responsible for accounting for every occurrence, you need not be overmeticulous about it. You are not running an entrepreneurial business. You have no profit-loss statement to produce. However, reasonable diligence and fiscal conservatism are required.

To emphasize the transitional role of the fiduciary estate, Figure 12.1 is presented. Some of the terms therein will appear in the final petition; others may not. The purpose of Figure 12.1 is to help you pull together those activities that are essential for preparing to close the estate. Keep in mind that your objective at this point is to *formulate* the distributable estate. You are not yet ready to make the actual final distributions.

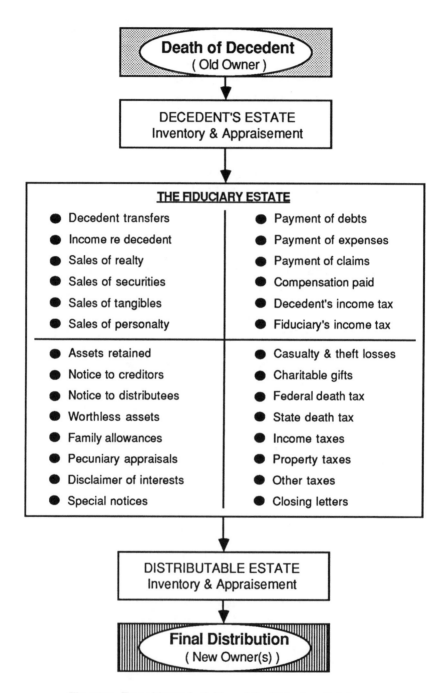

Fig. 12.1 - Transitional Activities of the Fiduciary Estate

Sales, Etc. Documentation

There are two schools of thought on the best way to manage a fiduciary estate. One school is to sell everything; that is, sell all noncash items, real and personal, and convert them into cash. The opposite school is to "sell nothing": simply keep everything the way the decedent left it. Each philosophy has advantages and disadvantages. As usual, reality imposes a compromise.

Selling everything (that can be sold) has the advantage that the estate is fully liquified. Distribution then becomes simply a matter of writing a check. The disadvantage is that some property items will be sold at what is perceived to be an unnecessary loss by affected distributees.

Selling nothing (except when cash is needed) has the advantage that the full market value of the property passes directly to the distributees. Each then makes his own decision whether to sell or not. Other than "paying the bills," the executor has very few decisions to make. The disadvantage is that there can be problems with titling the property at time of distribution. When there are three or more distributees of an estate, titling problems can become aggravating. And, invariably, at the last minute, some distributee will want cash instead of in-kind.

As executor, you have discretionary powers which are virtually unlimited. Certainly, you must follow the instructions of the decedent. But you are not required to consult with the distributees on every fiduciary decision that you make. Accordingly, we say: "Sell everything that you can."

Of course, use sound judgment. If there is only one distributee, the surviving spouse, for example, you certainly don't want to sell her home out from under her. Similarly, with fixed-income sources for retired distributees (time deposits, trust deeds, corporate bonds, etc.). Otherwise, sell everything that you can.

Obviously, you must document each property item that you sell. You start with its appraised value at time of death. You add to this all fixup expenses, improvements, selling expenses, and sales commissions (if any). You subtract the sum of these from the gross sales price, to determine your gain or loss. That is,

Gain (loss) = Gross sales price LESS (appraised value at death + fixup + improvements + selling expenses + commissions)

Unfortunately, there will be losses on some items. Promissory notes, trust deeds, limited partnership interests, tangible property (vehicles, equipment), run-down businesses, and the like are not readily marketable. They require deep discounting to get them off your hands. In general partnerships, closely-held corporations, and other business deals, usually some "buyout" agreement has been arranged for decedent co-owners. Buyouts are rarely at a profit.

Whatever you sell, go that extra effort and "keep a trail." Make all pertinent notes and records that you can. Collect all documentation into a **Record of Sales, Etc.** Segregate the sales into realty (land and buildings), intangibles (securities and notes), tangibles (vehicles and equipment), and personal effects (furniture and furnishings).

Other than real estate and marketable securities, you could turn everything else over to an auctioneer. That which the auctioneer can not sell could be given to charity. The point here is that you can get rid of most property items if you try. Memorabilia, of course, is the exception.

Don't be too upset if the net cash from all of your sales effort is considerably less than the inventory and appraisement at time of the decedent's death. This is bound to happen as part of the price the estate pays for achieving liquidity.

Set Up "Tax-Free" Reserve

Back in Chapter 2 (Figure 2.3 particularly), we urged you to set up an estate checking account with a financial institution of your choice. We urged that you run everything through that one account. We urged a *checking-only* account: one that does not pay interest. We wanted "no strings" on you for deposit balances, time delays, and frequency of check-writing. We wanted that account to pay on demand at all times. Please take a moment and go back and look at Figure 2.3; it is on page 2-14.

As you start selling off the assets of the estate, your account balance will grow significantly. When this balance starts to exceed, say, $10,000 to $15,000 or so, we suggest that you set up a *tax-free* reserve account for the distributees. Arrange for speedy transfers from the checking account to the reserve account. Depending on the initial gross estate, we can see this reserve account building upwards of $100,000 to, perhaps, $3,000,000 or more. This reserve account will be the primary asset of the distributable estate. Thus, now, you will have two accounts: the checking account and the reserve account (tax free). The two-account arrangement we have in mind is presented in Figure 12.2.

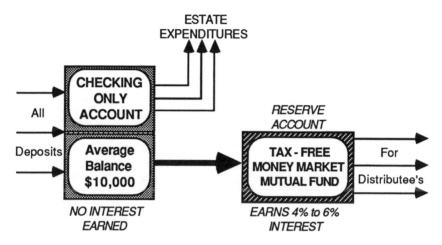

Fig. 12.2 - Closing Preparations for "Tax-Free" Distributions

What kind of tax-free reserve account do we suggest?
Answer: A no-load mutual fund of municipal bonds.
What's that?

A mutual fund is a regulated investment company whose investment objectives are public-noticed in a registered Prospectus. A "no-load" mutual fund charges no commissions upon purchases or redemptions. There is, however, a management fee. This fee is approximately 0.5% of the average daily assets under management (subtracted from the tax-free income). Municipal bonds are debt obligations of states and their political subdivisions issued to obtain funds for public purposes, such as the construction of airports, bridges, highways, housing, hospitals, mass transit, schools, prisons, streets, and water and sewer works. These debt obligations are backed by the "full faith and credit" of the issuing municipal agencies. They pay from 4% to 6% per annum interest. This interest earned is federally tax-free, and is tax-free in the issuing state as well.

Mutual funds are the best sources for participating in municipal bonds. This is because the fund management actively purchases and redeems these bonds in multi-million-dollar blocks. They buy diversification in 100 to 1,000 different municipal agencies. Many of these tax-free funds advertise regularly in financial journals and elsewhere. We urge you to investigate several of these funds, and select one of your choice. Then set up an estate account in the name of your decedent.

Most distributees will be absolutely ecstatic when you send them their final distribution checks, and you inform them that the amounts are federally tax-free!

Reappraise the Nonsaleables

If the decedent's will specifically provides that certain items of property shall go to specific distributees, said items cannot be sold arbitrarily by you. As such, they become "nonsaleable" assets in the fiduciary estate. They are earmarked for specific distributees; you cannot substitute cash for them.

However, should the nonsaleables comprise a large fraction of the estate and prevent you from paying all expenses, claims, debts, and taxes, you have no choice but to apply to the probate court for an *Ex Parte Order* directing the sale of one or more of such items. Nevertheless, you can sell only those items which are absolutely necessary for estate settlement purposes.

In many cases, you will still be left with some nonsaleables (directed by the decedent). Due to the lapse of time between date of death and date of distribution, some of the nonsaleables could diminish in value. Jewelry could lose in value, as could collectibles, antiques, securities, vehicles, business assets, land, and buildings. If the loss in value is significant enough, an intended distributee might accuse you of mismanagement. To protect yourself against this possibility, you should have all of the "final" nonsaleables reappraised. Use hired professional appraisers only.

For these reappraisals, an official probate referee is not needed. Simply look in the yellow pages of your phone book for those appraisers who specialize in the specific property items that you have on hand. Set a target date for the likely distribution of each item, and have the appraiser provide you with a certified statement of its description, condition, and value as close to the intended distribution date as possible. If appropriate, have the appraiser indicate the probable cause of change in value. The reappraised value — in documented form — becomes the backup to your accounting summary as you prepare to close the estate.

Prepare Accounting Summary

Tax accounting and estate accounting are two different worlds. In addition to the tax aspects that we have discussed, you will have to prepare a summary of all transactions that occurred in the fiduciary estate. You can start the preparation of this summary from that one check-writing account that we show in Figure 12.2.

Back in Figure 4.3 (on page 4-12) we suggested a coding arrangement for your deposits and expenditures. The coding system that we suggested then was to help you to identify and classify your day-to-day transactions. We wanted you to get in the habit of organizing your deposit receipts and cancelled checks. If you did not do the organizing then, we urge you to do so now. Bank deposit receipts and bank cancelled checks are "third party" records. As such, they are proof positive of your fiduciary transactions.

For estate summarization, we suggest the following categories:

Deposits

1. Decedent transfers
    - money from those accounts which were closed
2. Decedent's income
    - accruals during life but received after death
3. Proceeds from claims
    - life insurance, death benefits, trusts, refunds, etc.
4. Fiduciary income
    - income of all kinds (taxable and nontaxable) after death
5. Proceeds from sales
    - those assets sold in the fiduciary estate

Expenditures

6. Decedent's debts
    - charge accounts, payables, mortgages, etc.
7. Payment of taxes
    - death, income, property, sales, employer, etc.
8. Payment of claims
    - includes casualty and theft losses
9. Expenses of administration
    - office expenses, travel, certifications, etc.
10. Compensation for services
    - appraisers, accountants, attorneys, etc.

Summarize the above (or other) listings into a comprehensive one-page report. Show the total deposits and total expenditures. The total deposits minus total expenditures represents the *cash distributable estate* (or "net cash"). The net cash, of course, is the balance in the checking account plus all of that in the reserve account . . . in Figure 12.2.

Incidentally, many tax-free mutual funds offer check-writing redemption privileges. Before any distributions are made, we urge that you apply for this check-redemption feature. Your intention is that upon final distribution, you can close the reserve account and revert to the regular checking account for residuals and contingencies.

Alert the Distributees

The cash on hand plus the current value of the nonsaleables constitute the *distributable estate*. This is that point in time just before "final distribution." We displayed this state of affairs back in Figure 12.1. When the distributable estate is total dollar valued, you are ready to alert the distributees. You want to confirm their status and ask a few pre-finalizing questions.

Are all distributees still alive? If so, where does each live? Has his/her mailing address changed? Has his/her name changed? Is the spelling correct? What is his/her social security number? Does any distributee refuse his share, or any part of his share, of the estate?

If a distributee is deceased at the time you are ready to make distribution to him, you must ascertain his *successor distributee*. A successor distributee is one who is legally entitled to receive property belonging to a decedent distributee. Such a successor may be designated in your decedent's will. If such a successor is not named, you then have to look to the law of "intestate succession" in the state where the distributee last resided. Better yet, if the decedent distributee had a will of his own, then you establish contact with his executor. For your purposes, the decedent distributee's executor becomes your distributee.

In some cases, a living distributee may have received a predeath "advance" from your decedent on the distributee's share of the distributable estate. Such advance is usually in the form of a non-interest-bearing personal note. If in writing, the principal amount would have been included in the decedent's estate. At distribution, the note is cancelled. No actual money transfers to the advancee.

There is another situation that can arise in the distributee-alert phase of your duties. This involves retractions/redemptions (called *ademptions*) of bequests in a will. There are two forms of ademptions. One form is a gift before death of the specific item or amount of money designated in the will. The second form is a retraction of the item or money before death, either by disposing of it or by removing the money from the source of the bequest. Both forms of ademption have the effect of removing the property from the estate. The bequest left in the will is thus nullified. The affected distributee may not understand this. You will have to explain and clarify this for him.

Another clarification needed at time of distribution is a pecuniary bequest directed to a trust. A "pecuniary bequest" is one which can be satisfied wholly or partly by distribution of property other than money. Where a trust is involved, the trustee becomes your distributee. Proper titling of the money or property transferred becomes very important. This means that you must contact the trustee and get specific instructions

Your objective in this *distributee-alert* phase is to anticipate and clear away all of the "glitches" that may come back to haunt you after the estate is closed..

Prepare the "Final Petition"

Comes now that time to file your "final petition" for distribution of the estate. This petition is a summary restatement of the essential facts and circumstances that have transpired. At this point, any pesky problems should be ironed out. This petition is the beginning of the end of your executorial duties.

In some states, preprinted official forms are available; in other states, checklist type outlines can be obtained. We will present our own outline to help you through the forest.

The heading on the final petition is similar to any other petition that you may have prepared. We have given several examples previously, particularly in Chapters 3 and 4. The title on your final petition is—

PETITION FOR FINAL DISTRIBUTION

Those items to be mentioned in the petition are tabulated in Figure 12.3. We suggest you take a moment and carefully read down the left-hand column. Note that a total of 30 items is shown.

YOUR EXECUTOR DUTIES

ITEM	COMMENT
1. Petitioner's Name	Executor or administrator
2. Decedent's Residence	State & county jurisdiction
3. Date of Death	As per death certificate
4. Will Admitted	Date admitted to probate
5. Letters Issued	Date of letters testamentary
6. Notice to Creditors	Required by law : 4 mos. wait
7. Creditor Claims	Filings, dates, amounts (if any)
8. Requests for Special Notice	Names & interests indicated
9. Inventory & Appraisement	As per "official" appraisal
10. Family Allowance	Names & amounts (if any)
11. Preliminary Distributions	Names & amounts (if any)
12. Sales from Inventory	Items sold; proceeds received
13. Worthless Items	Description, condition, disposition
14. Statement of Account	Gross estate less expenditures made
15. Heirs & Legatees	Names, addresses, ages, relationships
16. State Inheritance Tax	Date return filed; amount paid
17. Federal Death Tax	Date return filed; amount paid
18. Decedent's Income Tax	Date return filed; amount paid
19. Other Decedent's Tax	Describe with receipts for payment
20. Fiduciary Income Tax	Estimated filing date & amount
21. Letters Trusteeship	For missing heirs & trust transfers
22. Letters Conservatorship	For incompetent distributees
23. Letters Guardianship	For distributees who are minors
24. Disclaimers of Interest	Items refused by a distributee
25. Escheat to State	For undistributable bequests
26. Compensation Requests	Allowances for attorneys & executors
27. Distributable Estate	Total net value available
28. Distributees by Will	Names, items, & amounts willed
29. Contingency Matters	Pending audits; additional expenses
30. Readiness for Closing	Amount withheld for closing

Fig. 12.3 - Example Contents of Petition for Final Distribution

We think this is about as complete as you could ever be. Not all items, of course, will apply to your case, but many will.

Most of the listed items are self-explanatory, especially when you read the right-hand column of Figure 12.3. A few, however, require additional explanation. These especially are items 8, 14, 24, and 29.

Item 8 (Requests for Special Notice). When notice to creditors is published in a local newspaper, any person interested in the estate may file a "request for special notice." This request may be for copies of any or all petitions, statement of accounts, inventory and appraisements, or claims against the estate. The term "any person interested" is quite broad and can lead to financial snooping into your decedent's estate.

Item 14 (Statement of Account). All probate documents become public record. This fact invites inspection by promoters and others who want an insight into the financial affairs of the distributees of the estate. Nondisclosure of these matters is possible by your requesting "waiver of account" in the final petition. Waiver will be granted if you were authorized to administer the estate independently, when you initially sought your letters testamentary.

Item 24 (Disclaimer of Interest). If a distribute refuses to accept an item of property or amount of money bequeathed to him, he must file with the court a written disclaimer thereof. Once he does so, the disclaimer is irrevocable. The property or money is thereafter assignable to other distributees.

Item 29 (Contingency Matters). In estate matters, nothing is ever final-final. There can be unforeseens and incompletions which hang on annoyingly. The most common are potential audits and recomputations of every tax return filed. Property or income may be discovered which was not included in the gross estate. And there will be certain "closing costs" which have to be anticipated. Therefore, a listing of the contingencies likely and the costs thereof, should be indicated.

Lastly, on the petition, you say that "The estate is in a condition to be closed." Then you add—

WHEREFORE, petitioner prays for judgment as follows:
1. That waiver of final accounting be allowed.
2. That the property be distributed as set forth above.
3. That all other proper orders be issued.

You sign the petition and verify, under penalty of perjury, that the contents are true, correct, and complete.

Final Notice to Distributees

As you surely understand by now, any time you file a petition in probate court, you have to provide opportunity for interested parties to attend a hearing thereon. This means sending out a final Notice of Hearing (Probate). Said notice is sent officially to all distributees of the estate and to each party, if any, who has requested special notice. Virtually every state court has prescribed official forms for this hearing notice.

The preprinted forms carry a bold-faced notice thereon to the effect that—

This notice is required by law. This notice does not require you to appear in court, but you may attend the hearing if you wish.

The notice goes on to read to the effect that—

NOTICE is given that _____ (your name) _____ *, executor of the estate herein has filed:*
      NOTICE OF FINAL PETITION
      (AND WAIVER OF ACCOUNT)
as per copy attached hereto.

The date, time, and place of final hearing is given, followed by the signature of the deputy clerk who has set the court calendar. The clerk also has to certify that he has posted the notice in a public place. This is usually on a bulletin board conspicuously located in the general public areas of the court house.

As executor, you have to send a separate photocopied form to each noticee, together with a copy of the petition. You must *mail* the notice. You cannot deliver it in person. After mailing to all noticees, you then execute "proof of service by mail" and submit this proof to the clerk for filing with your petition.

Since the noticees do not have to attend the hearing, it is suggested that you prepare an informal transmittal letter to them with an acknowledgment form attached. State in the letter that you have requested "waiver of account" in order to protect their financial privacy. Tell them that you will provide them each a statement of final account when you actually make distribution to them. Request that they sign the acknowledgment form and return it to you. Provide them with a self-addressed, self-stamped, return envelope for this purpose.

Make up your own acknowledgment form. Include such statements as—

1. I acknowledge receiving on _____ (date) _____ Notice of Hearing and Petition for Final Distribution.
2. I have no objection to granting the petition as prayed.
3. I have no objection to waiver of account as prayed.
4. I will ☐ will not ☐ attend the hearing as is my privilege.

_____ (signature of noticee) _____

If there are no objections and no attendees (other than yourself), the hearing is nothing more than a "roll call." The decedent's case number is called; the judge asks "any objections." He pauses a moment, then scribbles his signature on a document which he hands to the head clerk. The next case is immediately called.

If you lay all the groundwork properly, and get all the forms in order, there is no need for an attorney (in uncontested cases).

Judgment on Final Distribution

What the judge scribbled his signature on was his Judgment Directing Final Distribution. This is the final order of the court. It is recorded in official records and thereafter is available to you in the form of clerk's certified copies (for which you pay a fee for each copy). It is an order to close the estate and make distribution as directed.

Who prepares the Judgment Directing Final Distribution?

The judge does not prepare it; he signs it. The clerk does not prepare it; he records it. *You* prepare it. It is quite stereotyped and summarizes the key matters of your petition, in authoritarian form.

The preamble wording goes like this:

The petition for final distribution on waiver of account of (your name), executor, came on regularly for hearing by this court this date. Petitioner, (your name) , appeared without counsel. On evidence given to the satisfaction of this court, the court makes the following findings:

The findings in example form are presented in Figure 12.4. As you can see, they are a restatement of facts in your petition, in past tense form.

THE COURT FINDS THAT:

1. Notice of time and place for hearing has been duly given as required by law.

2. Notice to creditors has been published in the manner and for the period prescribed by law.

3. The inventory and appraisement of the estate, together with its accounting and report, are full, verified, true, and correct.

4. All claims filed and presented against the estate have been allowed, approved, and paid except as otherwise indicated for cause.

5. The State inheritance tax (where applicable) has been paid, and a duly countersigned receipt has been filed.

6. The Federal estate tax has been paid but a duly executed closing letter has not been received; thus, there is a possibility of additional tax.

7. The additional Federal tax, if any, should be assessed to each distributee in proportion to each distributee's share of the decedent's estate.

8. The executor and his attorney are each entitled to statutory compensation for their services.

9. The estate is in a condition to be closed. All debts and expenses of administration have been paid. Reasonable closing expenses should be allowed.

10. The property of the estate should be distributed as hereinafter ordered.

Fig. 12.4 - Illustrative "Findings" in Judgment on Distribution

After the findings are recited, there appears the judicial command:

IT IS ORDERED, ADJUDGED, AND DECREED THAT;

1. The administration of this estate is brought to a close without the requirement of an accounting.

2. The report and petition of ___(your name)___, executor for the estate of ___(decedent's name)___ is approved, and all acts and transactions of the executor relative to those matters in the report and petition are ratified and approved.

3. The executor is authorized to withhold the amount of $_____ for closing expenses and other contingencies. Any portion of that sum not so used shall be distributed to (residue distributee).

4. Should any death, income, property, or other tax return be examined, and additional tax found to be due, the executor shall assess each distributee in proportion to his share of the distributable estate.

5. ___(your name)___, as executor for the estate is allowed $_____as his statutory fee for ordinary services, and is allowed $_____ compensation for his extraordinary services.

6. The executor shall distribute all property of the estate as follows:

___(name and relationship of each distributee)_____

___(full legal description of each property item)_____

7. All other property of the decedent not distributed hereinabove, whether described herein or not, is distributed to (residue distributee).

Dated:_____   _____(signature)_____

Judge of the Superior Court

Note in two places above that we use the term "residue distributee." This is preferably one person, preferably mentioned in the will, who is to receive the odds-and-ends residue of the estate. The residue includes small amounts of leftover money, pennyworth securities, insolvent businesses, damaged property items, and other unwanted assets. These are classed as items of "no significant value." It is helpful that any and all residue be assigned to one person (or entity) so the estate may be totally closed.

Information in Distribution Letter

We recommend that you request ample certified copies of the final judgment order. There should be one copy for each distributee for his or her own personal records. If the estate has not been fully liquidated into cash form, there should be one copy for each piece of realty, each trust deed, each security, each registered vehicle, each business interest, and each depository account still in the decedent's name. And, of course, there should be one copy "for the file" and one copy for your own personal records as executor.

You write each distributee a letter, stating that the estate is closing and that you are forwarding his/her distributive share thereof. Attach a copy of the judgment order.

In the case of cash, cite the check number, date, name of bank, and its face amount. Inform the distributee that this amount represents his/her share of the distributable estate, as directed by the decedent.

If other than cash, attach a copy of the pertinent title to each property item distributed. Suggest that upon physical acquisition of the distributed property, each new owner thereof contact the proper authority for changing title of the property into his/her own name. In the case of vehicles, this means going to the state department of motor vehicles. In the case of stocks and bonds, this means going to a brokerage firm. In the case of real property, this means going to a title company . . . or to the County Recorder. And so on.

When distributing property other than cash, describe each property item with particularity, and cite its reappraised value at time of distribution. Also, cite its value at time of death and emphasize that the "death value" is the recipient's *tax basis*, should the property be subsequently sold, exchanged, gifted, or otherwise disposed of. It would be helpful to make reference to federal tax code Section 1014: **Basis of property acquired from a decedent**. Use such excerpts as—

The basis of property in the hands of a person acquiring [it] *from a decedent shall be . . .*
(1)   its fair market value at date of death, or
(2)   its alternate value at 6 months after death, or
(3)   its "special use" value authorized by Section 2032A [for qualified real property used for farming and business use].

Cite (1, (2), or (3), whichever is appropriate to the property item being distributed.

Include a statement in your distribution letter that, although all required death-related tax returns have been submitted, all such matters have not yet been closed. As per Paragraph __ of the Judgment Order, if any additional tax is due, it is assessable against each distributee prorata. Assign to each distributee his/her prorata percentage as determined from the statement of account for the estate.

Close your distribution letter by preparing a *formal receipt* for each distributee to sign. Repeat the description of each item of property. Include agreement to the assessable percentage, should additional tax be due. Request full legal signature by the recipient, and request return of the receipt to you (*not* to the court). Send your letter by Certified Mail.

When you receive the signed receipt(s) for all property distributed, the estate is no longer under your care. What happens to it from this point on is not your responsibility. The "new owners" take full charge. The transition from the decedent's ownership to the distributee ownership is complete.

When Closing is "Final"

When all distributee receipts have been returned to you, prepare one last petition to the court seeking an order discharging you from all executorial duties and relieving you of any further liabilities therewith. Attach the original distributee receipts to the petition, and keep photocopies for your own files. No hearing is required on the probate discharge order.

Do not confuse the probate discharge order with a tax discharge order. Probate proceedings and death taxes are two different legal worlds. Probate is a state law matter, whereas death tax is a federal law matter.

So, try as hard as you might, there is one matter that will delay your full discharge from all responsibility. It is that federal death tax return, Form 706, that you (may have) filed. Although you filed it on time and paid the tax, if any, your tax accounting liability does not end. It does not end until you receive from the Internal Revenue Service its **Estate Tax Closing Letter**.

It may take anywhere from nine months to three years to receive the IRS closing letter. This is because every Form 706 is manually examined. It is not mechanically processed like ordinary income tax returns. Manual examination is necessary because (1) greater amounts of tax per return are involved, (2) due dates are staggered throughout the year, and (3) there are more tax technicalities involved. So the government is going to take its time, even though you have completed all of your other duties timely and effectively.

You can speed up the 706 examination time by attaching a written request to the return when you submit it. Your authority for requesting expeditious handling is embodied in Section 2204 of the tax code. This section is headed: **Discharge of fiduciary from personal liability**. Subsection (a) thereunder reads in part as—

> *If the executor makes a written application to the* [IRS] *for determination of the amount of tax and discharge from personal liability therefor, the* [IRS] *... within 9 months ... shall notify the executor of the amount of tax. The executor, on payment of the amount of which he is notified ... and on furnishing any bond which may be required ... shall be discharged from personal liability for any deficiency in tax thereafter found to be due and shall be entitled to a receipt or writing showing such discharge.*

The "receipt or writing" to which Section 2204 refers is the IRS form Letter 627: Estate Tax Closing Letter. The substance of this letter reads—

> *Our computation of the Federal tax liability for the above estate is shown below. ... You should keep a copy of this letter as a permanent record ... to close the probate proceedings for the estate. This letter is evidence that the Federal tax return for the estate has either been accepted as filed, or has been accepted after an adjustment that you agreed to.*

Except for concealment of assets or for misrepresentation of material fact, Letter 627 closes the federal death tax issue. It cannot be reopened.

At this point, you can wrap up all your records and files and put the estate to rest. Put IRS Letter 627 on top. You are now finis!

ABOUT
THE AUTHOR

Holmes F. Crouch

Born on a small farm in southern Maryland, Holmes graduated from the U.S. Coast Guard Academy in New London, Connecticut. He received a B.S. Degree in Marine Engineering and served on active duty in the U.S. Coast Guard. While so serving, he wrote 15 technical articles on maritime matters for various trade journals. After resigning from the Coast Guard, he was employed as a technical writer and nuclear engineer in the Los Angeles and San Francisco areas. During this time, he completed 25 post-graduate courses at the University of California. He received an M.S. degree in Nuclear Engineering and a "Ph.D.—Almost" in Materials Sciences. He wrote two books, "Nuclear Ship Propulsion" (345 pp) and "Nuclear Space Propulsion" (430 pp), which were published.

As a consequence of these two books and the tax writeoffs therewith, his income tax returns were audited by the Internal Revenue Service (IRS). This annoyed him to the point where he decided to become a professional tax preparer. He studied for and passed a 12-hour written examination offered by the IRS. Thereupon, he became enrolled (licensed) as a private Tax Practitioner. He started his own business (tax preparation and tax counseling) in 1972.

Since that time, he has witnessed sweeping changes in the tax laws and their adverse effect on individual taxpayers. He has also witnessed that the IRS is **not** the industrious, impartial, and competent federal agency that its official public imaging would have us believe. He found that, under the slightest pretext, the IRS will interpret against a taxpayer, will assess maximum penalties, and will delay pending matters so as to extract the maximum possible interest on any additional tax due.

Disturbed by this willful misconduct of the IRS and by the general lack of tax knowledge by most U.S. taxpayers, he saw the need for an innovative, all-new, series of *taxpayer-oriented* Federal tax guides. To fulfill this need, he visualized a 25-title series of guidebooks for providing in-depth knowledge on one tax subject at a time. Selected subjects would be those which plague applicable taxpayers all 12 months of the year. Hence, his generic formulation of "Allyear" Tax Guides.

In 1981, he began writing the first title in his projected 25-book series. But before long, he ran into a legislative firestorm of major "tax reforms": 1982, 1984, 1986, 1988. After rewriting his manuscripts several times, he completed in 1988 an introductory set of five prototype tax books, namely:

103 — Tax Guide: GOING THROUGH DIVORCE
203 — Tax Guide: INVESTOR GAINS & LOSSES
303 — Tax Guide: WRITING YOUR WILL
403 — Tax Guide: SELLING YOUR HOME(S)
503 — Tax Guide: WINNING YOUR AUDIT

As can be seen *on the reverse side hereof,* each of these titles is the center book in each of five miniseries, comprising his 25-title project.

Addressing the post-1988 tax law changes, he instituted extensive desktop effort to have each of his tax titles on a computer diskette. But he did more than just manuscripting. He prepared each disk in **press-ready** book form: complete with all typesetting, graphics, editing, pagination, and text layouts. This makes more feasible his ongoing updating of vital tax information.

Holmes welcomes comments and suggestions from his readers, and especially their own direct experiences with the IRS. These inputs become his informational reservoir for future editions.

Holmes is married and has three adult children. He lives in Saratoga, California.

y

ALLYEAR TAX GUIDES

25 Titles Featuring " Knowledge Beyond "

Series 100 - INDIVIDUALS AND FAMILIES

101 - Tax Guide: BEING SELF EMPLOYED
102 - Tax Guide: CLAIMING TRAVEL EXPENSES
103 - Tax Guide: GOING THROUGH DIVORCE
104 - Tax Guide: TWO SPOUSAL INCOMES
105 - Tax Guide: CITIZENS RESIDING ABROAD

Series 200 - INVESTORS AND BUSINESSES

201 - Tax Guide: STARTING YOUR BUSINESS
202 - Tax Guide: RISKS WITH PARTNERS
203 - Tax Guide: INVESTOR GAINS & LOSSES
204 - Tax Guide: BANK & BROKER INPUTS
205 - Tax Guide: SIDE BUSINESS VENTURES

Series 300 - RETIREES AND ESTATES

301 - Tax Guide: WHEN YOU RETIRE
302 - Tax Guide: SIMPLIFYING YOUR ESTATE
303 - Tax Guide: WRITING YOUR WILL
304 - Tax Guide: YOUR EXECUTOR DUTIES
305 - Tax Guide: TRUSTS AND TRUSTEES

Series 400 - OWNERS AND SELLERS

401 - Tax Guide: RENTAL INCOME PROPERTY
402 - Tax Guide: LAND & OTHER RESOURCES
403 - Tax Guide: SELLING YOUR HOME(S)
404 - Tax Guide: ANIMAL BREEDING & CARE
405 - Tax Guide: SELLING YOUR BUSINESS

Series 500 - AUDITS AND APPEALS

501 - Tax Guide: KEEPING GOOD RECORDS
502 - Tax Guide: PROTESTS AND APPEALS
503 - Tax Guide: WINNING YOUR AUDIT
504 - Tax Guide: GOING INTO TAX COURT
505 - Tax Guide: TAX RETURN BALLOTING

NOTE: Not all titles above are currently in print. Contact publisher for catalog.